SELECTED WRITINGS, VOLUME I

Gender

MEN
WOMEN
SEX
FEMINISM

BY FREDERICA MATHEWES-GREEN

CONCILIAR PRESS
Ben Lomond, California

GENDER: Men, Women, Sex, Feminism

Published by   Conciliar Press
                  P.O. Box 76
                  Ben Lomond, California 95005-0076

Printed in the United States of America

ISBN 1-888212-31-4

Unless otherwise noted, all Scripture quotations
are from the Revised Standard Version of the Bible.

CREDITS:
Versions of some of these essays appeared initially in the following publications, sometimes under
different titles:

National Catholic Register, "Lunch with Frances Kissling"

Cornerstone, "Her Flesh and Blood"

Philanthropy, Culture, and Society, "A Labor of Love"

The Handmaiden, "Feminism's Next Generation"

World, "The Flaws of the Fifties," "Fraternizing with the Enemy," "Overthrown by Eros," "Born
That Way," "Monster," "Hotel Full of Cowboys"

Beliefnet, "Flowers for the Fellas," "What Really Motivates 'Anti-Gay' Conservatives?"

National Public Radio, "Perils of Pizza Delivery"

National Review Online, "Let's Have More Teen Pregnancy"

The following first appeared in *Books & Culture:*
"A Cab Ride with Gloria Steinem" (May/June 2000), "The Women of Disney" (March/April 1996)

The following first appeared in *Christianity Today:*
"Who's Taming Whom?" ("Men Behaving Justly," Nov. 17, 1997), "Men Need Church Too" (May
24, 1999), "Sex and Saints" (April 3, 2000)

The following first appeared in *Touchstone: A Journal of Mere Christianity:*
"Twice Liberated" (Summer 1994), "Three Bad Ideas" ("What Women Need," August 2001)

"Safe-T-Man" ("What's Wrong With Men?") is copyright 2002 Religion News Service. Used by
permission.

A form of "Why Humans Mate" appeared in the book, *Real Choices: Listening to Women, Looking
for Alternatives to Abortion* (Conciliar Press, 1997), as well as in *The Handmaiden.*

for my mother, Dorothy,
and my sisters, Louisa and Dorothy

CONTENTS

FOREWORD

SITTING DOWN TO READ a collection of essays and columns is a different experience from reading a full-length book on a specific topic or theme.

The latter is kind of like watching a movie. You know it's going to have a beginning, a middle, and an end—usually in that order. The images come at you one after another and, by the final credits, everything should make sense. It's all one big story.

A collection of columns or essays—such as this book—is something else altogether. It's something like a festival for short feature films on a common theme or even, at times, a display of fine photographs in a gallery. Each item in the collection has to make sense on its own, each telling its own complete story.

I have written a thousand or so news columns myself and I know how this works. The writer has to find individual stories and images that lead the reader to the bigger truths. All of those individual stories can, when placed side by side, create a larger story.

If the writer is good enough, all of the snapshots combine to reveal a bigger picture. If the writer is good enough, all of the little stories become part of a much bigger story. You just have to pay attention, looking for the themes that pop up over and over again in all of the individual stories. What ties all of these works together, of course, is the eye behind the lens.

Each of the essays and columns in this book was written at a very specific time, for a very specific audience, to tell a very specific story. Think of them as short films and snapshots taken during the past few decades in American life. Some of them are short and almost poetic. Others are newsy and packed full of information. Sometimes the stories overlap, since they are dealing with similar events and themes.

One thing is certain: These stories are replete with beautiful and haunting images that were captured with the help of a unique lens. Frederica Mathewes-Green simply sees things that other people fail to see. She hears voices that other people would like to ignore.

She doesn't sound like other writers because other writers have not lived her life, from countercultural unbelief to countercultural faith. She has the unusual ability to listen to abortion-rights activists and feminists because she once was one of them. She is the rare person who was actually paying attention during the late 1960s and remembers the good as well as the bad. She remembers when feminists didn't like Playboy or worried about the sexism woven into Disney movies. Her eye is clear, her voice steady, and her faith consistent.

In this day and age, that makes her seem like one strange and unorthodox lady.

Try to find another Christian writer today who would or could write this: "Women are just as much in need of salvation as men are. . . . Women bear the same moral responsibility men do. They face the same temptations. And, if they die outside the grace of Jesus Christ, they go to the same hell. It's compatible with an honored feminist principle—we don't believe in all-male clubs."

Try to find another writer who can start a page with poignant quotes from feminist poet Adrienne Rich and legend Germaine Greer, yet end up with this bottom line: "As the old cliché has it, girls give sex in order to get love; boys give love in order to get sex. When the sexual revolution flooded the market with 'free sex,' its trading equivalency in square units of love was radically depreciated."

Now, imagine someone offering that point of view to Gloria Steinem, Naomi Wolf, the seekers of Beliefnet.com, or millions of listeners on National Public Radio.

When it comes to the terrain covered in this book—"Gender: Men, Women, Sex, Feminism"—Frederica Mathewes-Green has been there and done that.

The good news is that she returned from the front line with a marvelous collection of snapshots. Put them all together and they offer a wonderfully fresh look at the story of our lives.

Terry Mattingly
Columnist, Scripps Howard News Service
Associate Professor of Mass Media and Religion,
Palm Beach Atlantic University

1 | TWICE LIBERATED: A PERSONAL JOURNEY THROUGH FEMINISM

WHEN I JOINED THE COLLEGE NEWSPAPER as a shy fresh-man many years ago, the editor gave me my first assignment: "Find out what's all this stuff about women's lib." I was baffled as to how to do that; reports of feminism (which was then usually called "women's lib") were just beginning to titillate the public, just begin-ning to show up in Johnny Carson jokes about "bra-burners." Was it possible to dig up any local "libbers"? My editor had a suggestion: go to the Student Union and have them announce over the loud-speaker, "Anyone representing the women's liberation movement, please come to the information desk."

It is interesting to imagine what would happen if such a mes-sage were announced from that same desk today. But in September 1970, there was a slight pause before two women came steaming up, glowing with the zealot's inner flame. Kathy and Rosa steered me into the student lounge, where they opened to me the hidden knowledge of women's oppression through the ages. As they ex-pounded this mystic wisdom, I began to nod. I liked what I was hearing.

I was ready to believe in something. I had spurned my Roman Catholic upbringing a few years before, and spent the high school years strumming anti-war songs at a hip Unitarian church. (Our elfin pastor was fond of repunctuating St. John: "God is. Love!") It was *deep,* of course, but somehow it wasn't enough, sharing superior smiles with the elbow-patch crowd and sneering at Nixon. We were pledged to reject any conviction more precise than that people are grand and everyone should be nicer to each other. I was seventeen, and I was looking for deeper convictions.

So when my first campus byline appeared a week later, it was over a story that cautiously endorsed the "libbers," and I continued my catechesis under Kathy and Rosa. The prototype-version of women's lib that they initiated me into was still searching for a focus. The movement understood itself as firmly underground, and was self-consciously counter-cultural, even deliberately crude. Wearing suits with little bow ties and carrying briefcases was the farthest thing from our minds. We ridiculed *men* who wore suits.

The movement was a spontaneous, uncoordinated explosion of energy and anger without a clear plan and, in our case, amply fertilized by ignorance. Childless, we talked about using communal baby-farms to free women from the awful burden of their own children. Sexual neophytes, we talked earnestly about the Myth of the Vaginal Orgasm. Naive girls' dorm dwellers, we sought out the town's lesbian bar, where we were invited to dance by very serious older women with arms like sides of beef. In my own body I displayed the confused zeal of the time: I stopped shaving my legs but continued plucking my eyebrows.

However, in a phase of the movement's life when it was associated with the term "man-haters," we generally got along well with men. Most of us remained cheerfully heterosexual. We were in league with our brothers in the hippie counter-culture, and our enemies were not men, but straights (meaning, in those days, non-dope-smokers), Young Republicans, Jesus Freaks, and the Establishment.

I snubbed would-be beaux who weren't sufficiently enlightened. When Gary Mathewes told me on our first date that, if he ever got married, he'd want to hyphenate his name too, I thought, "This might just be the one."

In my senior year a movement buddy stopped me in a hallway. She was ecstatic with the news: a woman had won a top executive job at AT&T, wasn't it great? No, I said, surprised at her enthusiasm. What do we want executive jobs for? That's just a way of being co-opted, getting sucked into the establishment. The women's movement is not about trying to get a bigger piece of the pie, I insisted. We're talking about a different kind of pie altogether.

Someone scheduled a debate for an empty classroom; I represented the counter-culture side. We're selling out, I said. We didn't start this revolution to end up with our representatives wearing tasteful jewelry and looking important on TV. Remember Joni Mitchell singing, "You could have been more than a name on the door on the 33rd floor in the air"? Remember Harry Chapin singing about the executive father too busy to see his son, and the son saying, "I'm gonna be like you, Dad"? Didn't we reject all that careerism and materialism as deadening to the soul? Why in the world would we want it now?

I don't recall if I won the debate; my position certainly did not win the war. As Naomi Wolf explains in her book *Fire with Fire,* the movement came to split between Victim Feminism (self-defeating poutiness and man-blaming) and Power Feminism, which she champions. Wolf cites core principles for Power Feminism: Retaliation, Money and Worldly Power, and Victory.

My search for something deeper was not going to be satisfied by a women's movement that lusted after worldly power; I was truly looking for a counter-culture. If I could have listened to my heart more carefully, I would have identified some of those revolutionary values as love, joy, peace, patience, kindness, and the rest of the Galatians 5 list. I searched in "new age" and age-old Eastern religions, but nothing really rang true to me, and the blue gods were never more than amusing.

A month after graduation, our hitch-hiking honeymoon brought Gary and me to Dublin. The late afternoon light was glaring as we stepped inside a dusty church and stood there blinking. I walked over to examine a white marble statue in the back: Jesus pointing to his Sacred Heart, which was twined with thorns and springing with flames. I remembered the words from Sunday school: "Behold the heart that has so loved mankind." A few minutes later I realized I was on my knees. When I stood up, I was a Christian.

In the following decades my relationship with feminism changed even as the movement itself changed. It took me several more years to question abortion, and longer than that to question the denial of gender differences. Gary and I attended Episcopal seminary and hoped to share a priestly ministry, although being a female priest was a difficult goal at that time; it ceased being my goal at all after Gary had been ordained a few years and I saw how hard the job is. (Later still, in 1993, we became Eastern Orthodox, and Gary became Father Gregory.) We still clung to the labels "feminist" and "liberal," though those identities were being gradually hollowed out and replaced. When Gary was finally compelled by pro-life convictions to vote for a Republican presidential candidate, he took along one of our young sons to actually pull the lever. He declared when he came home, "These hands are still unsullied."

I had come around to a pro-life position too, but didn't feel comfortable with the movement's "right-wing" image. When I heard of a group called "Feminists for Life," I joined immediately, and when they needed a newsletter editor a few years later I volunteered. At my first board meeting I received some surprising news: the editorship made me automatically a Vice President. What's more, this was the first time the tiny organization had ever had an officer living near Washington, DC. I was deputized to try to get some media attention for the organization. I was as perplexed about how to do this as I'd been years before, when commissioned to interview women's libbers. The other members of the board suggested that when something newsworthy happened, like a Supreme Court decision, I should go hang around and try to get on TV.

It was July 1989. When I heard on the morning news that the Supreme Court's Webster decision had been released, I put on my "Feminists for Life" sweatshirt—the only pro-life garment I owned—and we drove into DC carrying stacks of anti-abortion statements by Susan B. Anthony and other nineteenth-century feminist leaders. Clustered all over the marble steps and landings were knots of movement leaders, surrounded by knots of media people, and mobile TV transmitters towered high overhead. I gave a copy of my flyer to Molly Yard, who scowled at me, and one to Bella Abzug, who lectured me. Movement leaders had lined up, politely alternating pro-choice and pro-life, to give their thirty-second bites for a network camera, and I tried to gather the courage to join them. It was very hot. Gary observed, "Your sweatshirt is working."

After that things snowballed. I was invited to appear on a C-SPAN call-in show, the first time I'd spoken in public about abortion. A month after that I flew to New York to be on a brand-new show called "PrimeTime Live." I wrote opinion pieces and flew to speaking engagements and stood behind the podium at press conferences. Before long I'd assembled a video scrapbook: me wearing tasteful jewelry and looking important on TV.

But as the years passed, the old "feminist" identity began to rankle. I could wear the label by applying a vague definition that it meant merely the full human equality of women and men. Still, I was uncomfortably aware that the average person gave the term many more connotations. As my vocation had gradually become that of writer, I'd become more respectful of the power of words, and more committed to using them accurately. If I used the word "feminist" to mean something most people didn't understand, I wasn't communicating. It was dishonest. My work depended on using tools precisely, and employing an esoteric, private definition for any word amounted to damaging my tools.

I was having trouble with the concept, not just the label. The presuppositions of feminism seemed to divide, implying that issues pertaining to women could be separated from, were more important than, other issues. My view of the human condition and the pervasiveness of sin had broadened, leading me to the conviction that women could not ultimately win a better lot from any human agency, nor could their situation be improved without helping men and children as well. We are all together in this stewpot, and we all need the same Savior; He makes no distinctions between male and female.

I even began to think that the whole theory was erroneous— that in Western cultures men and women rise and fall together, their situation affected by race or class, seldom gender. An American housemaid has more in common with her short-order-cook husband and her bricklayer brother than with the wealthy female lawyer whose toilet she cleans. Of all the ways that genuine injustice can be discerned, gender came to seem increasingly inaccurate.

But most important, I began to see that feminism was bad for me. It inculcated feelings of self-righteousness and judgmentalism. It filled me with self-perpetuating anger. It blinded me to the good that men do and the bad that women do. It made me think that men and women were enemies, when we actually have a mutual Enemy, who delights in any human discord.

I began to suspect the whole thing was a self-serving sham. It was that we wanted to be victims too; in our culture, victims have power. Feminism allowed half the human race to claim instant victim status, no matter how much material comfort we enjoyed. It was powerfully seductive, and I was starting to think it was a lie.

After a few years of my representing Feminists for Life, *Christianity Today* asked me for an essay presenting pro-life feminism. I complied, but wondered if I was doing the right thing. When the editor requested changes making the feminist angle more prominent, I felt the screws tightening. I rewrote the piece, and as soon as I'd submitted it I phoned the Feminists for Life office and said I needed to resign. I could no longer call myself a feminist. The journey that had begun that day in the student lounge, as Kathy and Rosa eagerly expounded the faith, had come to an end.

SOMETIMES I'M ASKED, "How could you leave a progressive mainline church for the Orthodox Church, which is so patriarchal and oppressive?" My experience has been the opposite; the Orthodox Church has been much more welcoming of my gifts than the Episcopal Church ever was. I have been invited to write, speak, and preach in countless Orthodox venues; I never had such invitations in my previous denomination.

What seems to confuse outsiders is the issue of women's ordination. Yet that can't be an accurate guide to respect for women, as my experience proves. Even though Orthodoxy does not ordain women, it continues the historic pattern of honoring women saints, and these women did most of the things associated with a Protestant pastor. Women teachers, preachers, and theologians ministered to men and women alike: some went as lone evangelists to foreign lands, some ruled over entire nations, some were sought by both men and women as spiritual mothers. Historic Christianity has always recognized women's gifts, and recognized them in a natural, easy-going way, without making a big deal about it. Women saints are just saints, neither more nor less than men saints. Harping on that double X chromosome would seem to Christians of earlier centuries both obsessive and bizarre.

I'm also asked, "Is there anything that you gained from feminism that is worth retaining?" There are at least three "women's rights" for which I will continue to fight.

1. The right to be at home in our bodies. This means the right to have our bodies left whole and healthy, unaltered for any goal of social engineering or impossible ideal of beauty. Included under this heading would be the right to reject the killing of our unborn children as a ghastly false offer of freedom; as professor Sidney Callahan says, we will never climb to equality over the dead bodies of our own children.

Included, as well, would be chemical tampering with women's hormones—pills, shots, implants—to fit her for sexual use without commitment. While my church accepts non-abortifacient, non-surgical methods of birth control, there is a possibility that these methods cause miscarriage rather than truly preventing contraception. Even without that concern, these methods should be questioned. The lumps of Norplant rods, palpable under the skin of the upper arm, are as degrading as the metal tag in a cow's ear. There is also the unknown impact that the daily ingestion of artificial hormones can have on a woman's hormonally influenced emotions. My friend Julianne Wiley asks, "Why should I put chemicals in my mouth that I wouldn't put in my compost heap?"

I reject overly medicalized childbirth for much the same reason

I do abortion and chemical contraception. I taught prepared child-birth for years and had three unmedicated births, the last at home, and experience taught me that birth is as natural a process as breathing or digesting food. When the body is functioning as it is designed to do, there's no need to intervene in the name of speedy efficiency. The birth attendant's role should be like that of a lifeguard, who watches out for trouble but does not jump in the water and pump swimmers' arms for them. Not every woman will choose an unmedicated birth, but every woman should be allowed an un-meddled-with birth.

On a less serious note, being at home in our bodies means accepting our natural body shapes, colors, and textures, and rejecting pathetic attempts to alter them to fit an impossible ideal. Cosmetic breast, belly, and facelift surgery is sad, and futile rebellion against God's good design. I frequently see women self-subjected to illogical, uncomfortable standards of appearance. Is it my old feminist roots that makes me want to give them this advice?

- Do not spend large amounts of money fighting wrinkles, or large amounts of time fighting your hair. Even if you just keep your hair clean and brushed and otherwise let it do what it wants, you will still be allowed to vote and own property. Wrinkles tell the story of your life. Don't try to falsify the story; instead, write the story you would want others to see.

- If there is a big difference between the ways you look before and after you put on makeup, you're wearing too much makeup. Your goal is to like your face just as it is right out of the shower. A smile is your best ornament, with more impact than anything you could spend on jewelry, makeup, hairstyle, or clothing. The best way to make your eyes more beautiful is to spend more time in prayer.

- Do not spend time strangling in pantyhose, teetering on heels, or otherwise distorting your body without asking yourself, "Is there an easier way of dressing that will be equally acceptable in this situation?"

- Go ahead and buy larger clothes. Imagine a composite of all the women all over the world who share your age and childbearing history. Apparently that's what God has in mind. It's okay to look like that.

- Think about the distinction between "beautiful" and "attractive." Attractive people are the ones you are drawn toward; they attract in the sense that magnets do. Many components go into attractiveness, but beauty is not necessarily one of them; some beautiful women are cold and bitter and actively repel. Beauty inevitably fades, but true attractiveness can be forever. So cultivate attributes that you find attractive, which as St. Peter tells us have to do with the "hidden person of the heart" (1 Peter 3:4).

2. The right to be different from men. Early feminism insisted that men and women were just alike. Later a strain arose that insisted that they were different: women were perfect and men were bums. Neither position is helpful.

It seems to me that men and women are alike in the overwhelming majority of categories (think of the number of body parts, internal and external, that the sexes have in common). The differences seem more noticeable because we are used to comparing ourselves with each other, not with other creatures. We ignore what's alike and accentuate the differences.

Some feminists would assume that where the genders differ, they are in conflict. It seems more likely that gender differences are meant to fit together. This is demonstrably true in the physical realm, and emotional and temperamental differences as well may be designed by God so that in coming together they balance each other and create a harmonious society.

For example, a popular theory holds that men and women differ in their approach to moral questions. Women, it is said, begin with the human context, asking who will be harmed and who helped, and seek to improve the home community. Men, instead, begin with principles of justice, and seek to conform the situation to those ideals. (Of course any individual man or woman will exhibit a mix of these approaches, but in theory most people favor their gender's end of the scale.)

It is tempting to consider man the norm and woman a variation, but we are more interdependent than that. Neither end of the pole should outweigh the other. When a society is overly ruled by masculine, principled justice it loses touch with mercy, and an iron code is applied to the warm flesh of human relationships. The ideal good becomes a Procrustean bed on which hapless limbs are stretched or sawed to fit. This is exemplified by Javert's obsessive pursuit of Valjean in *Les Miserables*, and culminates in the miserable excesses at Nuremberg.

We have no trouble recognizing the dangers of "masculine" moral excess, but are not as quick to perceive the "feminine" extreme. When principles shred away and leave a feelings-driven ethic of situational response, we quickly discover that the unconverted human heart is a ruthless place, increasingly eager to rationalize and kill in the name of compassion.

How can this be? It follows a subtle evolution: what begins as suspending the rules so that everyone can be happy becomes (in the face of that impossibility) disregarding the rules so that I and mine can be happy. That possessive is appropriate: the protective tigress draws the circle ever smaller, until finally the woman regards herself alone as the just beneficiary of any choice she makes. In her classic *In a Different Voice,* Carol Gilligan described the process in tones of admiration: a woman's moral development begins with self-interest, then opens to include other's concerns, then ultimately matures, Gilligan said, to include once more her own best interest. As I read the case studies she supplied, it seemed to me that the last level of maturity looked nearly identical to the selfish first.

Thus, we hear some on the fringe of the pro-choice camp admitting that of course abortion kills a baby, why shouldn't women make life-and-death decisions? When a woman is charged with killing her own children, we can count on some feminists to say that this is proof of the stress of motherhood and oppression of women's roles. Without objective standards to measure against, acts of horror can be romanticized into proof of female suffering and nobility. This is the inevitable culmination of feelings-based morality untempered by masculine justice. It ends with Emma Bovary destroying those who love her in her craving for a dramatic life; it ends with Scarlett O'Hara trampling over those who love her in her craving for money. It ends with a prostitute standing before a judging king and saying to a desperate mother, "Neither you nor I shall have him. Cut him in two!"

Unrestricted abortion on demand is the clearest example of where a sentimental, me-first moral order goes when it is not balanced by masculine-flavored insistence on principle. Both ends of the pole are necessary. When women are restricted from contributing their balance of mercy, a thousand slaves are crucified on the road leading to Rome. When men are restricted from contributing their balance of justice, women tenderly, privately kill their own children.

3. The right to go to hell. A corollary of the above morality is that a woman can't be really, really bad; if she does something bad, it's someone else's fault, and proof, in fact, of her oppression. "Victim Feminism" has embraced the not-quite-logical but extremely useful notion that a victim is always sinless. This constitutes a "Get out of jail free" card, sometimes literally.

However, a saying from my earlier feminist days would contradict this view: "The pedestal is a prison." When we treat women with extra indulgence, we actually demean them. We pretend that they are not really as strong or competent as men. They are slipped into a lower moral class, like that of minor children, and presumed non-culpable because they didn't know what they were doing, or were so emotionally overwhelmed they couldn't help it. This treatment ultimately trivializes them.

Women are just as much in need of salvation as men are. While women and men have many delightful differences, there is one item we indisputably share: "All have sinned and fallen short of the glory of God." When we hear the term "lost sinner" we seldom imagine the face of a woman, and when a lovely young thing sings "Amazing Grace," we may have to squint a bit to recall that she is still "a wretch like me." We aren't used to imagining John the Baptist leveling his "brood of vipers" speech at a group of women, or to visualizing female adherents of the Pharisee party condemned by Jesus as "whitewashed sepulchers."

Yet women are just as worthy, and as in need of, such rebukes as men. Just as women can share in nearly every physical affliction that affects men—God does not reserve for them only the dainty diseases—so also they are as susceptible to the gravest spiritual diseases and sin. Certain patterns of sin may appeal more to one gender than another, but for every sin the wages is death. Women bear the same moral responsibility men do, face the same temptations, and, if they die outside the grace of Jesus Christ, go to the same hell. Real feminists hate all-male clubs.

AS A CHILD, I WAS A CHRISTIAN, and as an adult I'm a Christian again. But in the middle I was something else: a feminist. Some would say there's no contradiction, that Christians can be feminists, since Jesus came for men and women equally.

That's not where I disagree. In the old pre-feminist jokes, women would frustrate men in argument by saying, "It's not what you said. It's the way you said it." I could use that line here. It's not so much what feminists say (well, with secular feminists, sometimes it *is* what they say), but how they say it. It's that attitude of self-righteousness. A tendency to pull rank as a "victim." A lack of humility. A blindness to the fact that women, just as talented as men, are just as sinful, too. Smugness, touchiness, judgmentalism; and toward men, even darker notes of condescension, ridicule, and anger. Pretty much the opposite of every line in 1 Corinthians 13. My brothers and sisters, you did not so learn Christ.

This, finally, constitutes the most serious of my reasons for renouncing feminism. It's not what you say, as long as what you're saying is that men and women stand on level ground at the foot of the Cross. It's how you say it—that superciliousness, that snide twist. That attitude is a grievous spiritual disease, and it will block the healing and transformation that is ours in Christ. Women captured by this attitude may well succeed, acquire money and power, and win the whole world—at the cost of something far more dear.

2 | THREE BAD IDEAS

FEW BOOK TITLES have had the sticking power of Richard Weaver's *Ideas Have Consequences*. Even people who've never read it find the blunt title instantly compelling. Weaver's thesis was that the ideas that we absorb about the world, about the way things are or should be, inevitably direct our actions. Though the book was published in 1948, before many current bizarre ideas had fully emerged, the thesis is an eternal one. It sets people to wondering which ideas were the seeds that sprouted our present mess, and which new ideas might be helping us out of it—or further in.

Ideas about the nature of life combine in a framework which can go by many names. Perhaps the word *paradigm* has become annoying through overuse, but some equivalents would be *worldview, mindset, outlook, ideology, cognitive framework*, or *reality grid*; a New Testament term is *phronema*. Whichever you choose, it means that mental assumptions link together and result in actions—ideas have consequences.

A few decades ago, some people got a bad idea. Or perhaps the bad idea got them, and shook and confused them till the right ideas came to look strange. We might trace it to the Supreme Court's Roe *v.* Wade decision, in January 1973, but even that document grew out of prior ideas. It didn't stand alone, and it cannot be combated alone. I'd like to explore three interlocking, mutually supporting bad ideas that sprouted during that era, and then look at some ideas about how to fix things.

It's hard to pin down exactly when these bad ideas sprouted, but I can point to the moment when I first encountered them in bloom. As a college freshman, I embraced early-seventies feminism with the eagerness of a cult devotee. I use the language of religious conversion intentionally. Just as conversion to Christ confers an entirely new way of looking at life—the *phronema* of the Spirit— feminism offered me a whole new worldview. I had rejected my childhood Christian faith, but feminism offered membership in a parallel enlightened community, one that had sacred writings and advanced leaders able to instruct neophytes in the vision. Initiates met in ritual gatherings—consciousness-raising groups—where we used a vocabulary unique to insiders. We had distinctive clothing and grooming styles; in our own way, we had a tonsure and habit.

It wasn't long before I became a leader and teacher myself, a member of the inner circle and a guru of campus feminism. This proto-feminism wasn't identical to the one prevalent today; the earlier version was full of energy, but unclear on direction, and shooting off in multiple directions at every imaginable target. Not all the ideas popular then continued to be part of the movement. Of the ideas that lasted, not all were successful. Of the ideas that were successful, not all were bad.

For example, one idea that died quickly was that women should live in community and pool their children in a cooperative caretaking scheme. This didn't happen, because once we started having kids we discovered that we didn't really like how other people wanted to raise them. We wanted our own separate homes, and personal control over child-rearing decisions. Doing it by community vote turned out to be impossible, and the cause of too many arguments.

Here's an idea that had some tenacity, but didn't succeed. One of the things that I found most provoking in those early-feminist days, and which became a favorite crusade, was the way women's bodies were used in advertising. I know it sounds crazy, but back in those days ads actually used images of sexy women to sell wholly irrelevant products, like toothpaste or cars. As we said—as we said *constantly*—women were being exploited as sex objects.

Those who think feminists were victorious in every battle and now control the world should turn on the TV, or open a magazine, and estimate how much progress this cause has made. This is one battle that most feminists finally abandoned as unwinnable. It turns out that you *can* fight City Hall. What you can't fight is Madison Avenue.

A happier idea was more successful. It was that women should return to more natural standards of physical appearance and give up arduous fakery. You may not recall how bizarrely artificialized the ideal of female beauty had become by the sixties. Perhaps it had to do with the space race or the fad of modernity, but everywhere women started looking squeezed and plasticized. Rent a film from that era and notice how armored the women's bodies look, how rigid and exaggerated their figures, how vast and immobile their hair, how surreal their makeup. Remember bright green eyeshadow swabbed up to the eyebrows, and shiny white lipstick? Real women don't look like that; even these women themselves didn't look like that stepping out of the shower. Starlets had to be assembled every day by a squadron of assistants, like a portable tank.

These wallpapered Amazons contrasted with more natural beauties of earlier decades, like Katharine Hepburn or Bette Davis. Likewise, compare a fully fortified Ursula Andress of 1965 with Julia Roberts or Sandra Bullock today, and you see a real victory for women. Only a few women burned bras, but all of us threw away our girdles, and as a result the world is a friendlier place. The idea that women's natural bodies are beautiful enough was a good idea, and the consequences have been good as well.

But some ideas were bad, and the greatest producer of grief, of course, was abortion. I lose track of how many millions have died; when it passes forty million the mind begins to swim. We can cope with such figures only by ignoring them. Once I heard someone observe that a memorial similar to the Vietnam Veterans' memorial, listing the names of all these babies, would have to stretch for fifty miles. That was many years ago, and it would be many miles longer today. But such a wall cannot exist, because those babies never had a name.

We think of abortion as the defining, litmus-test issue of feminism, but it was not always so. When the massive anthology *Sisterhood Is Powerful*, the feminist bible, was published in 1970, only one portion of one essay focused on abortion. (By the way, that essay debunked the phony scare-statistic that 10,000 women died annually from illegal abortion: "It is no longer anywhere near the truth and has no place in any serious discussion.") In 1967, when the National Organization of Women met for the first time, abortion and contraception were mentioned only briefly at the end of its "Bill of Rights"; *abortion* appears only as the last word in the document.

Abortion was far from the most important feminist issue. But among a number of bubbling ideas, abortion rose to the top, I believe, mostly because it was concrete. How could you measure whether something as foggy as "respect for women" was improving? It was impossibly vague. But repealing a law, or passing a new one, was a tangible goal. You could make a plan to achieve it, then implement and correct the plan, and have something to assess at the end of the day. Legalizing abortion was practical, and as a result it became important.

Much the same thing happened in nineteenth-century feminism, as voting rights for women overshadowed the more indefinite goals. Once the vote was won, in 1920, feminism went into suspended animation for fifty years. It was revived only by the reappearance of another practical goal.

There are two other bad ideas from seventies feminism, which combine to create a current situation that makes abortion seem indispensable. Think about it this way: Abortion is the solution, so to speak, to the problem of pregnancy. But when, and why, did pregnancy become a problem? Throughout most of human history, pregnancy has been a blessing. New children were welcomed, because they built the strength of a family and became the support of a couple's old age. New children mean new life; they mean both personal delight and growth of the tribe.

But for some reason, in the late twentieth century pregnancy came to seem an unbearable burden. It became so unbearable that one-fourth of the times it occurred, women sought abortion to escape it.

Was this because pregnancy had become dangerous to women's health? Was the nation wracked by war or famine? No, America during this period was the wealthiest, healthiest, most secure and comfortable nation in history. Pregnancy became unbearable due to a twofold change in expectations about women's behavior— two bad ideas. One was the idea that women should be promiscuous. The other was that women should place career above childrearing.

Both ideas were promoted by the feminist movement, yet there is a profound irony: Both ideas are stubbornly contrary to the average woman's deepest inclinations. Both ideas, in fact, were adopted unchanged from the worldview of the folks feminists claimed to hate—male chauvinists.

There is a pop-sociology concept called "imitating the oppressor," which means that when a group struggles for a new identity, it tends to adopt the values of whomever it perceives to be holding power. Thus, anything that looked "feminine" made feminists uncomfortable, because in the opinion of men it was weak. Why we should think that men were smarter than our mothers and grandmothers was never clear. Most of the time, we acted as if men were made only a little higher than pond scum. Yet we accepted unquestioningly that a man's life was the ideal life. Everything about men seemed more serious, more important. We felt embarrassed at our soft arms, and betrayed by our soft emotions. Motherhood was a dangerous sidetrack, a self-indulgent hobby that could slow you down. That's the way men saw it, and who were we to argue? Whatever men treated with contempt was contemptible; whatever men valued was valuable. And what men valued most was success.

Though I use the term *careerism* to identify this value, I don't mean that women shouldn't have careers. I mean by *careerism* rather a half-conscious ideology which holds that the most important thing in life is the rank conferred by a place of employment. It's as bad for men as it is for women.

Careerism is a foolish idea on many levels, not least because only the most fortunate, and elite, people get to have careers. Most people just have jobs. When I was a young feminist mouthing off about how I was going to be out in the workplace and not stuck at home, my dad gave me a few wise words that, improbably, sunk in even then. He pointed out that most of the people in the world don't get their fulfillment from the thing that gives them a paycheck. They get their fulfillment from other facets of life: faith, family, hobbies, literature, music. For most people, a job represents only the hours they must spend each week to earn the free hours in which they can do the things they really care about. Careerism is the misguided notion that work trumps everything else.

In another odd twist of history, in the late fifties and early sixties there had been a groundswell of concern that careerism was a poison, and too much obsession with the corporate ladder was deadening to the soul. Brows were knit over "the rat race" and "conformity," "the man in the gray flannel suit" and "lives of quiet desperation." Early hippies recognized this anxiety and urged instead that we "drop out," get back to the land, make pottery and eat acorns. The early feminism I knew had a mother-earth flavor that meshed with that, but within a few years the movement was swept with longing for worldly success, banging on the glass ceiling demanding to be let in.

So feminism concluded that men, despite being idiots, were on-target about how we should live our lives. If men thought that housewives were dumb, that staying home and raising kids was mindless drudgery, it was so. It didn't matter that our foremothers for generations had found homemaking noble and fulfilling. What did they know—they were stupid housewives! We were embarrassed by our female ancestors and envied the males. They had power, and we wanted power. We couldn't imagine any success except success in men's terms.

Thus, feminism unconsciously adopted the very values of the people they claimed to be opposing, because it's so easy to get confused about what you really want. We ignored the evidence of our own eyes. We saw men losing their identities in their careers, exhausted in the "rat race," nourishing ulcers at three-martini lunches, and dying early of heart attacks. Yet we clawed to gain the same privilege. Even the painful absence of our own daddies from our childhoods didn't cause us to question this goal. It was the "sour grapes" principle in reverse: the grapes might look sour, but as long as men wanted them, we'd choke them down.

Abortion is the first bad idea, and careerism is a second; it forms a supporting layer, because competing in a man's world required that women be as child-free as men are. A third bad idea contributes to the picture, that of what we called "free sex." It occurred to people that it would be fun if everybody had as much sex as possible with as many people as they could. This is a theory that has not proved true in practice, but it maintains a tenacious hold.

This notion, of course, has been a favorite with men for quite awhile—the last few million years, perhaps. But its formal expression goes back to *Playboy* magazine, when the thesis was dignified with the audacious label "the Playboy philosophy." (The busts line up in a dusty old library: Socrates, Plato, Aristotle, Hefner.) In the early seventies, *Playboy* was a clearly identified enemy of feminism, due to its "exploitative images." That changed; *Playboy* is now an ally of feminism because *Playboy* is such an enthusiastic defender of abortion. You can put two and two together on that yourself.

There isn't a venerable history of women celebrating promiscuity; if anything, women's wisdom over the ages taught that emotional security was the precondition for sex being fun, and a wedding ring was the best aphrodisiac. But, again, what did stupid old housewives know? Men called them prudish, so that's what they were. Thirty years later, women are still going morosely out into the night in dutiful pursuit of fun. And if it's not fun, she presumes, it must be because something is wrong with her.

This is another way that women adopted unhealthy male values: They began thinking of sex as a contest or power play rather than an act of vulnerability and intimacy. Young women were encouraged to be sexual aggressors, and to think of themselves as free agents who could take up and discard men at will. They quickly noticed that men were amusingly helpless when lust was provoked, much more than women are, and their ability to elicit this helplessness made them feel powerful. An extreme example of this is the topless dancer, who commands the attention of a roomful of men, all of whom seem to be at her mercy. But as an ex-dancer once told me, "I had to ask myself, if I have all the power, how come I'm the only one in the room who's naked?"

When sex is linked to a sense of thrilling power, man and woman are enemies, not allies. They use each other to prove their prowess, to make a conquest, to score. These locker-room terms reveal how tense and combative this view of sex is. But women's traditional view of sexuality—indeed, the healthier view—is that it is inherently an act of risk, a willingness to be naked, vulnerable, perhaps even foolish, to expose what is unlovely as well as what is treasured and dear. This risk is only possible when both man and woman are pledged to love and honor each other. Then sex is indeed a coming-together, a union of whole persons and not just isolated parts. But the idea of sex as love-making has been replaced by sex as contest, and even young girls are invited to dress provocatively and test how powerful they can be. Power-based sex may be exciting, but its essential foundation is mistrust; its theme song is "My Heart Belongs to Me." No wonder the sexual revolution has been accompanied by so much divorce.

Earlier we asked, "How did pregnancy become unbearable?" These two bad ideas, careerism and promiscuity, come together like two sides of a vise. If the modern woman is dutifully promiscuous, a high proportion of her sexual experiences are going to be in a context where the male partner feels no responsibility for a resulting child. Indeed, a pregnancy is likely to seem to him a failure on her part, if not an injustice. Contraception has fostered the ignorant expectation that sex has nothing to do with reproduction, but sometimes raw biology still wins out. This woman may have far fewer pregnancies than her great-grandmother, but any one of them is more likely to be disastrous.

Likewise, if she has adopted the idea that professional work is more important than child-rearing, pregnancy can dynamite her life plans. The trick of juggling motherhood and career is so difficult that it's still material for magazine cover stories thirty years later. We're no closer to solving the problem, and I doubt thirty years more will help. For her great-grandmother, however, it's likely that one more baby would not create a significant burden in a life already arranged to accommodate home and children.

Thus these two bad ideas come together, pressing in inexorably, and making a woman feel she has no escape but abortion. Feminism sought, first, increased access to public life and, second, increased sexual freedom. But that participation in public life is greatly complicated by responsibility for children, and uncommitted sexual activity is the most effective means of producing unwanted pregnancies. This dilemma—simultaneous pursuit of behaviors that cause children and that are hampered by children—finds its inevitable resolution on an abortion table.

Feminists defend abortion with desperate passion because the whole shaky structure of their lives depends upon it. Indeed, Justice Blackmun in the Webster decision wrote that women had "ordered their lives around" abortion, and the Casey decision was based on the assumption that abortion had become a necessary part of the social machine. There's a sad accuracy in that. When something like abortion becomes available, surrounding expectations regarding reproduction and child care subtly shift to accommodate it, and eventually it appears to be indispensable.

This is why the fight against legal abortion cannot stand alone. If we could padlock all the abortion clinics tomorrow, we'd see the next morning a line 3200 women long pounding on the doors. We wouldn't have solved the problems that make their pregnancies seem unbearable. We wouldn't have changed the context that normalizes promiscuity and undermines a woman's authority to say no. We wouldn't have restored respect for the profession of mothering, or respect for fathering for that matter, so that men would be proud to love the moms and support the children whose lives they begin.

These three interlocking bad ideas present a complicated picture, and initially a depressing one. If you've ever played the game of pick-up sticks, you know how impossible the task looks at the beginning, when you must gradually and carefully dislodge the first sticks one at a time.

Yet pregnancy care centers across the country have been working on these problems for many years now, ever since the first Birthright was founded in 1965. There are estimated to be three thousand pregnancy care centers across the nation, in comparison with only a few hundred abortion clinics. Over the years these centers have shifted and enlarged their focus, so the early years' emphasis on the baby grew to encompass the pregnant woman as well, and then both the woman who had already experienced abortion, and young people who can be encouraged to make better choices.

Here, then, are three good ideas, and these ideas also have consequences. The first is to support the pregnant woman. Pregnancy care centers offer pregnancy tests, maternity clothes, medical referrals, practical advice, spiritual counsel, and many other kinds of aid; recently, many centers have become freestanding medical clinics and provide full prenatal care.

Yet the most important thing pregnancy centers provide will always remain the individual friendship support that a pregnant woman needs. When I began research for my book, *Real Choices: Listening to Women, Looking for Alternatives to Abortion*, I had the goal of discovering the main reasons women had abortions. I thought that if we could rank-order the problems women faced, material, practical, and financial, we'd be able to address them more effectively.

To my great surprise, I found that these practical forms of support were only secondarily important. Over and over, each woman told me that the reason she'd had an abortion was that someone she cared about told her she should. The people she needed to lean on for support in a crisis pregnancy, like her boyfriend or mother, didn't supply that support, but instead encouraged her—and sometimes, sadly, coerced her—to have an abortion instead.

While pro-choice advocates present abortion as an act of autonomy, pregnant women experience it rather as a response to abandonment. Pregnancy is the icon of human connectedness, binding a woman to her child and the father of the child. Abortion shatters those connections and leaves her desolate.

Thus, when I asked women, "What would you have needed in order to finish the pregnancy?" over and over they told me, "I needed just one person to stand by me." While there are many useful ways centers can support pregnant women, the most important thing they can give is friendship, simple moral support. Across the nation, pro-lifers are doing many important things to protect unborn life: making TV commercials, proposing bills in Congress, writing books. But the one thing that can prevent an abortion tomorrow is what women told me they needed: a friend. Individual, personal care for pregnant women is a very, very good idea.

A second good idea is that of offering grief counseling for post-abortion women. You might think that once a woman has had an abortion, it is too late for a pregnancy center to be of any help. The opposite is true. Nearly half of the abortions done each year are done on women who have already had an abortion. In a single year in California, almost 1700 women had two or three abortions.

Psychologists say the mechanism works like this: A woman has an abortion, but in her heart grieves for her baby, and unconsciously feels obligated to have another to "make up for" the one that was lost. This is called an "atonement baby." But when she "slips up" and becomes pregnant again, she finds she's still in the same bad situation. Circumstances are no more welcoming to a new life than they were before. She has a second abortion, and then has *two* atonement pregnancies to make up. It is vital that trained counselors help women work through their grief and come to a healthy resolution, so this cycle can come to an end.

A third good idea is preventative: to reach young people before they have become sexually active and give them resources and incentive to remain chaste. The best programs address young men as well as young women, and go beyond "just say no" to present the positive aspects of marriage. Some secular programs target girls alone, and counsel abstinence only till high school graduation; they may even drill girls to be suspicious of boys and believe they can't be trusted. This, I think, is exactly the wrong approach. If we want strong marriages and healthy two-parent families, we shouldn't be intentionally teaching mistrust. We need rather to raise young men who are trustworthy, and inspire them with a vision of the nobility of fatherhood. We need to enable boys and girls to behave in admirable ways, deserving of trust, rather than planting further suspicion between the sexes.

The best character education programs build boys into young men who will see in marriage the opportunity to take on a challenging and time-honored role. In our culture men are almost continually insulted, and conservatives and pro-lifers are not immune to this infection. Pregnancy care workers can find it easier to send a woman to the welfare office than to explore whether the father of the child might be called on instead. We expect these men to be "bums," and they live down to our expectations.

Pro-lifers easily speak of God creating new life, ordaining that the woman and unborn child be knit together, and they should recognize that God has appointed a third person in that situation as well. I wince when I hear pro-lifers say "she found herself pregnant"; it sounds like Victorian euphemism. It's as if the woman just discovered the baby in a parking lot. No, she had help with that project. For every "unwanted" pregnancy, there is a dad who needs to be challenged to do the right thing, for his own sake as much as his new family's.

Restoring young men to the role of husband and provider is the most important long-term strategy for reducing the need for abortion. If he is there, problems look much less dire. If he is there, she can do it. If she is alone, the struggle is much more steep.

Three bad ideas have intertwined their roots and created an array of bad consequences, with the loss of tens of millions of unborn children only the most bloody result. Destruction of trust between men and women, decline of marriage, rise of sexually transmitted diseases, and other ill effects will remain uncounted until the passage of centuries gives some historian perspective to comprehend the full sweep.

From that perspective, I hope, he will also see the counter-forces of health at the moment of their emergence. These forces are there, because, like the human body, a human community has an impulse to health. There are already encouraging signs that younger people, in their teens and twenties, are more pro-life and more pro-chastity than older folks. They remember having both mom and dad at work all day, and want to make more time to raise their own kids. At this moment we can see only the beginnings of hope, and not how it will all come about. But someday we will have that eternal perspective and be able to see how our few and feeble efforts might have prevented some evil from advancing, or even turned it back a few feet. May God give us courage; may He give us encouragement; and may we be brave enough to respond.

3 | IN A BOOKSTORE
WITH NAOMI WOLF

I REALIZE THAT MY HEART is pounding fast. I'm standing in the aisle near the checkout counter at the Politics & Prose bookstore in Washington, listening to Naomi Wolf give a reading from her new book, *Promiscuities*. I'm standing in my black patent heels and electric-blue suit, overdressed in the midst of all these people in soft cottons and jeans; when Naomi phoned to invite me to her "book party," I imagined something like a cocktail party full of important people where I would have to look smooth and talk good.

That would have been intimidating enough. This is intimidating in a different way, and I'm somewhat surprised to find that I feel nervous. I feel like someone caught at the wrong place at the wrong time, and in danger of being exposed and expelled.

An overflowing crowd has gathered for the evening, filling all the folding chairs and forcing latecomers like me to stand back in the aisles. It's hot. Naomi is trying to hold a hardback copy of her book open in one hand and a microphone in the other, and I'm wondering why there wasn't a more practical arrangement, a podium, a lapel microphone, or a mike stand. I have a home-handyman's fascination with figuring out more practical ways to do things—to sort laundry, balance a checkbook, keep a grocery list. I will evangelize on my discoveries to friends and even strangers until forcibly discouraged.

Naomi and I are kind of an odd couple, brought together by the abortion issue. A year ago we gave a joint presentation at a pro-life/pro-choice Common Ground conference; the title was, "Critiquing Your Own Side." We met a couple of months before at Kramerbooks Cafe to get acquainted and do a little planning.

I felt a tremendous affection for her right away, because she was so nervous. She said later that it was the first time she'd met a real pro-lifer face to face, and she had felt pretty edgy. She sat across from me at a small iron table, picking at a fruit plate, asking a ceaseless stream of questions. I thought she was charming. I'm drawn to nervous people—not the petulant and demanding ones, but the blurting-confessing-retreating-embarrassed-revealing-shy ones. The kind of person who has a little electronic message board running across his or her forehead reading, "Oh no, I shouldn't have said that." They elicit in me a motherly desire to console and calm and protect. I find this kind of person nearly irresistible, and sometimes wish I was more like that, more transparent and unguarded.

Not that Naomi appeared to need any protection. I knew from the way she had handled the tart criticism of her essay in the *New Republic*, which recommended rethinking pro-choice rhetoric, that she was one of those people with a hunger for truth so consuming she would walk through fire.

I lean an elbow on a bookshelf and try to take the weight off my silly heels. I do feel out of place. I'm surrounded by titles about Vedantic wisdom and gay vegetarianism and women firefighters. Even what I would agree with here somehow seems advanced in a challenging manner designed to exclude me. It's what I think of as the liberationist tone of voice, that cry of resistance and struggle against oppression.

And who is the oppressor? I think it's me. It's frustrating to be assigned this role and given no way to escape it. I'd prefer a neutral space where we could talk and I could explain my convictions, clarifying and describing. In Common Ground, I often said, our goal was to work through misunderstanding so we could arrive at genuine, sincere disagreement.

But most times folks don't want to understand. They prefer the enemy to retain the familiar assigned shape. It's a shame. The notes on the bulletin board, the rings in noses and defiance on faces, all make me feel cowed and excluded. Even sad.

It's the sadness of being misunderstood, a childish sadness, helpless, voiceless. I know how negatively conservative Christians are usually viewed. The fact that I don't overlap with that company completely is irrelevant in these broad-brush environs; even in those places where I do fit that mold, our actual beliefs don't match the jeering version of our convictions commonly assumed here.

It's not the first time in history this has occurred. Rumors about the early Christians were even more bizarre, and their fate even more extreme. In the martyrologies of the first few centuries, saints are always going to their deaths insisting that, no, they don't treat incest as a sacrament; no, they don't eat babies. The poor victims of Lyons (AD 177) noted that the abominations they had been accused of were so heinous that, not only would they not do them, not only would they not even think of them, but they didn't think it was even physically possible that people *could* do them.

A young woman near me is wearing an "Uppity Women Unite" button. I wonder, are those still around? Don't I have one in the collection in my button box, from about thirty years ago? Does my being here outnumbered in this crowd, a devout Christian, a pro-life advocate, constitute being uppity? Part of me affirms this, with self-righteous self-pity, but another part recognizes how counterproductive such emotions are.

Sad to say, in the opinion of that button, I probably don't qualify as a woman at all. If I'm pro-life, I'm the oppressor. It's depressing how thorough this prejudice can be. I met a woman through Common Ground who was an abortion clinic administrator, and she told me something intended to be conciliatory: "I always presumed that pro-lifers just wanted to defend patriarchy and oppress women, but I'm gradually coming to believe that some of you actually *do* care about babies."

It took my breath away. I thought we'd already made it past that step and were trying to climb to the next one. I thought everyone knew pro-lifers cared about babies, but thought we "only" cared about babies and ignored women. My goal was to show how much pro-lifers do to support women in need. Looks like that's a premature task. It was like thinking you were at the marathon starting line and finding out you were in the wrong town.

My efficiency-analyzing software gets triggered again during the question-and-answer period, as the crowd protests every time that they couldn't hear the question. Naomi tries to solve this problem by exhorting the audience to shout out their questions. This does not work. People asking questions are frequently self-conscious and reluctant to attract yet more attention, and this is especially true here because the questions are about sex. It always seems more practical to me to summarize and repeat the question. This gives me a chance to clarify an often-rambling comment, helps me make sure I've understood the point, and also buys time to think about a response. And it slows things down a little, which can be a blessing. When discussion is heated, getting through a question-and-answer period can feel like standing in a hail of bullets.

As the question period ends, I wander back to greet Naomi. She greets me warmly and invites me to join her crew next door for

dinner at the Thai restaurant. We pour into the tiny place and surprise the staff by asking them to put together a table for twelve.
Once seated, we give a simple order—bring us enough of whatever
is good—and begin sipping at some excellent Thai beer.

Naomi will leave the next morning on a book tour, and one
dinner guest asks whether every author gets to make such a trip.
No, Naomi says, only the lucky ones, and I add that I never did.
Naomi adds, "Yes, a lot of excellent books get ignored, and a lot of
foolish ones get more attention than they deserve."

This is typical of her generosity. She is kind at heart, and sincerely seeking. I don't know how to make any headway in this hostile culture except this way: by finding people who are willing to
listen, and beginning to talk with them, one at a time.

4 | A CAB RIDE WITH GLORIA STEINEM

A JOURNEY OF A DOZEN BLOCKS begins with a single step—in my case, stepping into the front seat of a cab on the Harvard campus while Gloria Steinem stepped into the back. My eyes were still red from crying. How I got there is another story.

In October, 1999, Harvard Divinity School and the John F. Kennedy School of Government cosponsored a conference titled "Core Connections: Women, Religion, and Public Policy." Admirably, the conference's organizers tried to include in the mix women that don't usually get invited to such shindigs, such as evangelical Christians. To recruit these attendees, Ambassador Swanee Hunt, director of the Women and Public Policy Program at the JFK School, enlisted the help of her sister, June Hunt, evangelical author and host of the Hope for the Heart radio broadcast. A third sister, Helen Hunt (not the actress, but director of the Sisters Fund), provided funding for the conference.

During the conference, the two dozen evangelical women who attended would meet in the hallways and over coffee to chat. Yes, we seemed to constitute only about ten percent of the participants. Yes, the plenary and panel speakers were heavily weighted toward a perspective different from our own. Yes, reflexive disdain for evangelicals kept popping up during question-and-answer periods, so much so that none of us felt comfortable getting into the question lines.

Nevertheless, we could tell the organizers and other participants were trying. There was a genuine desire to broaden their awareness of the range of political and religious viewpoints women bear. Most slights were not intentional, but more in the nature of oversights— simple unfamiliarity with others' beliefs. All in all, it was good to be there.

Friday night I participated in a small group discussion led by Sylvia Ann Hewlett about her findings regarding the despondency high-achieving women have over their childlessness. The setting gave me an opportunity to hold forth on some of my cranky ex-feminist ideas. I explained that I thought feminism went astray in the mid-to-late seventies, when it abandoned its early hippie "mother earth" style. Though naive, that strain of feminism at least affirmed women's domestic and child-rearing lives. Later "power feminism" adopted the contrary view, that housewives were stupid and that value came only from corporate success. Ironically, this was exactly what "male chauvinists" thought; feminism adopted a contemptuous male attitude toward women's work and rejected that which our foremothers had found honorable and fulfilling. (Of course, the male model— that career comes before all else—has never been all that healthy for men, either.)

Helen Hunt happened to be present in this small group, and told me afterward that she was very intrigued by my comments (though, frankly, I don't know if they were all that original). As we parted that evening she said, "Feminists need to hear from you on this."

The next night the closing plenary speaker was Gloria Steinem, and I arrived late, as usual. The place, a small amphitheater, was jammed. One solitary seat was open, right in the middle of the front row. I settled in there next to my friend, Lilian Calles Barger of the Damaris Project, and we prepared to hear a legend speak.

The speech was a bit nonlinear and seemed to be coming nearly off the top of Gloria's head; as she turned pages we could see they were handwritten in pen, as if recently dashed off. As she spoke of the confluence of religion and politics, it became apparent that Gloria is of the school that religion is a resource to be reinterpreted and reinvented. Indeed, this seemed to be the governing presumption of the conference. The presumption is that we should explore the spiritual realm and discover what best pleases and supports us, and discard the rest. Spirituality is a powerful resource that women have too long neglected, they would say. Much of it is stale and patriarchal, though, so we must sift through it to select those elements that seem true and right to us.

Some of us who were attending the conference—not just the evangelical Christians, but possibly also the Buddhist nun in her habit, and the Muslim women in their veils—see things differently. We believe that we are inheritors of a faith tradition that is coherent, rich, and profound. We have no desire to tamper with it. Instead, we want to listen attentively to it and learn.

These ancient faiths, because of their continuity over centuries, have achieved a multicultural validation that is worth respect. Communities widely separated by geography as well as time have lived their lives exploring these beliefs, and found in them cause for awe. This cumulative wisdom is something that no single one of us, trapped as we are in our own cultures and wearing our own blinders, is smart enough to second-guess. We might explain our disagreement with the "buffet" school of spirituality, then, by saying that we respect the witness of generations of women and men before us, and come to our faiths as followers and disciples, not as critics or shoppers.

But Gloria was on an entirely different track, one which seemed the broadly accepted starting point of her audience. She is still very striking: tall, slim, and dressed that evening in form-fitting red. Everything about her is long, even the palms of her large hands; her very long fingers were accentuated by a coiled-snake ring. She stood behind the podium at ease, enjoying herself, offering an analysis of religious themes and trends in an amused tone. The audience adored her.

There I was, sitting front-row-center, my knees about six feet from the podium. I noticed after a while that I was gradually feeling more and more besieged. I felt slyly insulted; things I held dear were being sneered at. I slumped down and leaned toward Lilian. My mind wasn't quick enough to come up with responses and explanations for everything Gloria was saying. Her comments were being received enthusiastically. I felt very lonely.

About this time we hit the low point of the evening. Gloria began describing an interpretation of church architecture that she had read, which drew parallels between the various structural elements and female reproductive anatomy. You can imagine what the church door and narthex and center aisle represented. This, I thought, was just silly. Then she completed the analogy by saying that the altar was the womb, "the site where childbirth takes place."

I felt slapped, and then quickly felt very, very sad. Lilian must have had the same reaction, because she threw her arm around my shoulder and held on like she was drowning.

Why did this image wound me, when so much of the rest could be dismissed with, "Oh well, she just doesn't understand"? Never mind that the analogy was inaccurate; as an old natural-childbirth teacher, I'm pretty sure the birth itself would transpire on the church steps. The problem with the analogy was not its confused view of female anatomy, but its obliviousness to the original, deeper meaning of the altar. Ignorant, cavalier, it didn't care to listen to what the altar meant to the people who built it, or those who had worshiped there for millennia.

It wasn't the altar that was being insulted, I felt, but Jesus Himself. The altar for me is the place where I remember Jesus' sacrifice for us, His torture and death, His overwhelming love and willingness to give everything for our sakes. What I heard instead was that Jesus doesn't matter, His love is forgettable, His suffering is invisible. All the nails and blood and thorns were obliterated in favor of a cheap giggle. It seemed to me one more example of the feminist narcissism that sees everything as being about women, and cannot see suffering and sacrifice if it is done by men. Jesus' broken body on the cross? Shrug. Let's be naughty, and talk about wombs instead!

I tried to choke them back, but tears started trickling down my cheeks. I felt so sad. The person I loved most had been insulted and trivialized, and I could do nothing. For the rest of Gloria's speech I sat there, thinking about this and leaking slow tears. I hoped she couldn't see me, though I was right in front of her and only a few feet away.

When Gloria finished her speech, Swanee Hunt stepped to the podium to say she'd been watching body language during the talk, and while some in the audience appeared energized, sitting up straighter and looking more alert, others had been "wilting." She reminded the audience that everyone should be respectful of others' beliefs, and to remember that we might be talking of things that others hold sacred. Think how you would feel, she said, if a speaker at the podium said lesbians were going to hell.

The kindness of these words had an effect the previous

mockery had not, and I started to cry in earnest. Something had been released, and now I couldn't stop. Snuffling and sobbing, right in the middle of the front row, parked under the podium, with no way to escape. Through 45 minutes of question-and-answer I sat there gulping back sobs, feeling like a conspicuous idiot.

As the crowd dispersed I wandered around till I found my roommate, Caroline Langston. We went into the ladies' room where we talked it all out, and I finished boo-hooing and washed my face. By the time we came out everyone else had gone, and we stepped outside into the cool early evening air.

Just as we were going across the lawn we came upon a small knot of people discussing whether to walk or take a cab across campus to the banquet that was next on the schedule. There stood Swanee and Helen Hunt, Divinity School Dean Anne Braude—and Gloria Steinem.

Helen immediately called me over and had me shake hands with Gloria. Swanee commented quietly, "Frederica is one of the ones who was wilting." (I could have hugged her for that.) Gloria looked at me frankly and said, "I didn't mean to hurt anyone." I replied, "I know that is not what you intended to do."

Helen then suggested that I come along in the taxi with her, Gloria, and Anne for the short ride to the banquet; Swanee and Caroline would walk. So we crammed into the cab, me in the front, Gloria in the middle of the back with Anne and Helen on either side. The cab was dark and seemed cavernous, with a Plexiglas shield that effectively segregated me and the driver from the others way in the back. I looked at the photos of the driver's children, illuminated by the dashboard lights. As we pulled away from the curb, Helen's voice came from the back seat: "Frederica, tell Gloria your critique of feminism. Gloria, this is so interesting!"

Picture it. My critique of feminism, in five minutes, for the elucidation of Gloria Steinem. From the front seat of a cab, no less. I turned around to peer through the little round opening in the shield. Gloria's face hung in the dark like a disk, large, pale, and impassive as the moon.

My sympathies at that moment lay all with her. She was probably thinking, "Here's some kook I never heard of, who was crying all through my speech, and now she's going to deliver a thumbnail criticism of my entire life's work."

I figured the best thing I could do in the circumstances was tell a story. I recounted a scene from my own feminist college days: I had been attending a consciousness-raising session at the home of lesbian friends and had gone upstairs to use the bathroom. There I discovered that the bathtub was full of cow manure. Why? "We're trying to raise psilocybin mushrooms."

This, I said, was a very different kind of feminism from the one we're familiar with now; this was not a kind of feminism that was going to climb the corporate ladder. For all its foolishness and flaws, mother-earth feminism resisted the idea that power-seeking and masculine-style careerism was life's highest goal. I could remember the day a friend told me enthusiastically that a woman had been made a vice president at AT&T, and I responded, "Why is that good news? We're not fighting for a bigger piece of the pie. We're after a different kind of pie altogether."

But "power feminism" won the struggle, I said, and Gloria interrupted me to say she'd never heard the term "power feminism" before Naomi Wolf coined it. I said that feminism had made a mistake as well in adopting another unhealthy male value, promiscuity, as liberating. Gloria interrupted me again, to say that others would charge feminism with being anti-sex, rather than promiscuous, because it opposes pornography. I couldn't see any way to get past this Ping-Pong game to real discussion, not in a cab in five minutes. It was a relief when we pulled up to the dining hall and I could politely sidle away.

Months later I got a second-hand message that Gloria was very sorry to have hurt me. I don't doubt that it's true, and know that I must hurt people, myself, sometimes, by trampling without realizing it on things they hold dear. Probably she still doesn't know just why I was hurt, or just chalks it up to Christians being generally parochial and touchy. I hope someday we have an opportunity to talk further. But not through a Plexiglas porthole.

5 | LUNCH WITH FRANCES KISSLING

DOES THE U IN U STREET stand for Ugly? It unrolls, grey and broad, across Washington's northwest, clogged with snuffling trucks and drifting bits of trash. Set back from the street is a handsome refurbished building. I pause inside the lobby to check the letterboard for Catholics for a Free Choice; there it is, alongside the National Abortion Federation and the mysteriously named "Greepneace."

I am going to meet Frances Kissling for lunch. She and I had been invited to a national Common Ground meeting; when some pro-lifers objected to Frances's inclusion, we were both disinvited. I had impulsively phoned Frances and suggested the two of us have our own meeting.

CFFC's offices are handsome, with old brick walls and gray carpets. Frances greets me in her corner office, its walls displaying black-and-white photos, a caricature of herself in bishop's robes, and a blue Mexican folk-art snake hurtling down the wall.

She appraises me warily, as cautious as a deer on the edge of a glade, and yet talks about herself continuously.

As we leave the building I make a lighthearted reference to the "Greepneace" sign; Frances furrows, startled. Yes, she admits, Greenpeace has an office here. I point out again the misspelling.

She doesn't get it. I'm afraid she thinks I'm making obscure fun.

A couple of doors away we settle into a trendy cafe. Frances slides into the banquette and I perch on a chair opposite her, my face reflected in the mirrored wall. Throughout our lunch Frances talks and talks. Throughout our lunch I pray. I remember all the prayers I said this week, usually prompted by my amazement for setting up this lunch. I prayed that I would be patient and loving. That I would be a good listener and able to let go of my agenda. I prayed for Frances—recalling that she, as a daughter of the Church, has been baptized, has taken Communion, has been claimed by God. From the mirror I surround Frances with whatever fallible love I have.

In her stream of words I hear determination born of ancient pain. A beloved relative was forbidden Communion after making an unacceptable life decision. To a child, the loved one deserves first loyalty, and the Church appears cruel, insensitive, grinding out the hearts of those who struggle to do right by their best lights.

The argument that abortion is a moral choice because the woman *decided* to do it strikes many as the most infuriatingly specious. What does *deciding* have to do with it? Does anything we do get sanitized if we think about it first? But the nobility of individual conscience is Frances's motivating force. She has utter trust that women (men too? everybody?) are able to make responsible decisions; that further, by a fuzzy alchemy, any decision a woman makes is moral. Arguments that abortion is bloody violence, that women choose abortion in sorrow for lack of better choices, that the mound of tiny broken bodies has not won us liberation, all must crash to pieces on this rock: *but she **decided** to do it.*

We talk about my Real Choices project, which seeks to discover the reasons for abortion and possible solutions. I invite her input and that of pro-choice colleagues. She can think of fewer and fewer

56

reasons to accept this invitation, winding up with the unassailable charge that pro-lifers are behind it. I speak of going down the road together however far we can, in the name of helping women. She refuses to go anywhere with anyone whose view of womanhood is (she believes) intrinsically negative.

At last I ask, "What makes you a Catholic?" She answers, as if echoing my prayer, the Sacraments. It is the Faith, the Church—she accepts classic Catholic theology, to the surprise of many allies. It is the moral teaching she finds repressive. I am pondering, as we leave the cafe and say goodbye at her building, the mystery of God's claim on a person, a life-long claim marked by the fragile sign of sprinkled water. How easily wiped away; how impossible to erase from the memory of God. "See," the Hebrew prophets remind us, "I have carved you on my hand."

As I turn on the ignition, the radio bursts to life; the Christian station is broadcasting "Bible Reading Fellowship." A sonorous male voice reads, "And David said to Saul, 'Why do you listen to the words of men who say, "Behold, David seeks your hurt"? The LORD gave you this day into my hand, and some bade me kill you, but I said, "I will not put forth my hand against him." See, see the skirt of your robe in my hand, which I cut off, but did not slay you . . .'" I ponder non-violence toward the unborn, non-violence toward our enemies. I turn toward the beltway with tears in my eyes.

6 | HER FLESH AND BLOOD

A FOOT, A RIB, A WOMB. A piece of glass. Whalebones smoothed and polished, netted in cloth. The mother takes her daughter's hand.

The girl is dizzy; bright sunlight stripes through the shutters and dims her eyes. The old cloth tape is in her mother's hand. A pause of disappointment; her waist has still not met the mark of 20. The whalebones that stripe across her bones, the bones of the dead behemoth, are stronger than her bones. Her bones are young and they will give. She pauses between small tastes of air. On the day she was born her waist measured 16 inches. The bones press in. The mother thinks: this hurts, yes, but this is the way the world is. Not to do this would hurt my daughter more.

Though she is still a very little girl, the mother has brought her, this bright day, to the old woman. The root of springing desire that can lead a woman to ruin must be cut out before it awakens. The sun on the grass is dazzlingly green and hot. The other women join them; they hold the girl down, many strong hands, and in the old woman's hand the glass is sharp, but not quite sharp enough to be swift. The little girl is screaming, higher screams flung higher, like red rags of banners cast into the air. The blood on the green grass is hot. The strong hands are firm and not without love. The little banners float higher still, still unheard, and disappear. The mother thinks: this hurts, yes, but this is the way the world is. Not to do this would hurt my daughter more.

Because the child's foot is so young, it rolls, it rolls more easily. The mother unwraps the cloth and finds the foot beginning to conform, beginning to meet the shape of its binding. She bathes it. The foot is pale, and in places the swaddled skin has been crimped into tiny folds like crepe. The tiny toes, once lined like peas, are beginning to splay under, to meet their new configuration. The mother is young herself, and frail. When the child drops her painted ball it rolls, it rolls out of reach; she lunges, but does not try to run, to retrieve it. The mother thinks: this hurts, yes, but this is the way the world is. Not to do this would hurt my daughter more.

The clinic waiting room floats with gray April light; heavy rain streaks the windows, flushes seeds from their beds to the gutter. The room is too small for the restless girl. Her limbs are long, still growing, but a second bloom is on her: roses riot in her cheeks, creamy light flows from her skin, her hair is thick, her waist thickening in blind eagerness to welcome the new daughter within. The mother sits across from her, feeling very old. A dozen years ago the girl sat on the third step smacking loud kisses on her doll's half-bald head; today she is silent, all the protests washed out of her. The mother sees, in the girl's hand, the tiny teddy bear she carries with her keys. The girl rubs the matted fur softly, but her eyes pierce the floor with hot, yearning tears. The mother, the grandmother, thinks: This hurts. Yes. But this is the way the world is. Not to do this would hurt my daughter more.

7 | A LABOR OF LOVE

THE TOUGHEST THING ABOUT MARILYN Szewczyk isn't her name. You can forget everything you learned in grammar school and rattle off "Seff-check." Keeping up with Marilyn's determination, energy, and vision is not so easy.

Marilyn arrives late for our lunch appointment, her ample silhouette filling the door. Outside it is a blistering white summer noon; inside, darkness and plush chairs. She makes her way to the table leaning lightly on her cane, souvenir of the stroke two years ago. The waitresses know her ("Hiya, Marilyn, hon, howya doin'?"). Marilyn asks for a table for three; she has scheduled a *second* luncheon meeting with someone else later. Marilyn doesn't have a lot of spare time.

Once seated, she begins laying out on the table her luncheon necessities: a smoky-transparent pill case, with yellow, orange, and gray pills; an insulin injection kit; a pack of cigarettes. A cigarette comes first; as the blue smoke curls overhead, Marilyn's latest meeting has begun.

Few would begrudge Marilyn the title of the Mother of the Pro-Life Movement in Maryland. As this state has dealt with the abortion issue over the decades, she's always been near the front lines.

But most of her energy goes not into fighting to make abortion illegal, but into working to bring women hope and help. Abortion is a grim, unhappy choice. Marilyn believes that, by offering shelter and clothing and a kind word, she can help women make a happier choice, one they (and their babies) can live with. Over and over, she's been proved right.

"I was pro-abortion when *Roe v. Wade* was decided," she says. "I thought it was a matter of religion: you know, 'Mine says it's not OK, yours says it is.'" Then a friend showed her photos of children in the womb, four weeks, five weeks, before the earliest abortions are done: tiny limbs blooming out like rosebuds, a heart tripping fast as hummingbird wings. "There's no way anybody could say, 'We don't know when life begins,'" she insists. Her gravelly voice is touched with simple sweetness. "That was life. There's no question when life begins."

By the mid-seventies Marilyn was volunteering with several of Maryland's pregnancy care centers. These centers offer pregnancy tests, material aid, and emotional support to women who decide to continue their pregnancies. Largely staffed by volunteers, the centers give away free whatever services they can offer, and whatever material help they can gather, to help women choose life. In all, there are about 3000 of these centers across the nation; by contrast, there are about 450 specialty abortion clinics, charging $300–350 for an average abortion.

Pregnancy care centers are an admirable embodiment of the early seventies slogan, "Sisterhood is powerful." The fight to defend or defeat legal abortion is no doubt overpopulated with male lawyers in suits; when women think about the issue, they are more likely to picture a friend in tears. While the political players thunder that abortion is a callous convenience or right, these women think it's something else: a tragedy. Few women want to have an abortion. Who would want to undergo an expensive, awkward, and humiliating medical procedure, and gain from it only the death of her child? If pregnant women find themselves faced with that last choice too quickly, it is because other women have not reached out with love and support, filling in more first choices at the top of the list. The more these other women think about pregnant women's sorrow, the more they think about the little torn bodies going into clinic dumpsters each day, the less they feel they can do nothing.

Pregnancy care centers operate on the venerable American tradition of barn-raising: neighbors help neighbors in need, and the job gets done. Since there is no income from clients, everything must be begged and borrowed. A typical center will have a lending closet of second-hand maternity and baby clothes, perhaps some baby furniture, a list of a few doctors willing to take on another charity patient, a list of families willing to take in a pregnant guest. One local grocery donates diapers and another gives some formula; a church pays the phone bill and a benevolent association covers the electricity. And, every month, the rent must be scraped together with donations from friends who've been asked too many times before.

Contrast this with the businesslike approach at the abortion clinic down the street. Here there is a commodity which can be sold, and over 1,500,000 are sold each year. At three hundred dollars per abortion, the proceeds near half a billion dollars; add in the much higher fees for late abortions, about ten thousand of them per year, and the figure rises dramatically. No wonder the providers of abortion can afford salaries, office space, even full-page ads in major newspapers and magazines. The pregnancy center director can just afford to run off "We can help!" flyers at the local quick-copy, then thumbtack them to the bulletin board at the laundromat.

But can they help? How much good can a pregnancy center do? When a pregnancy is difficult, there is usually a tangle of reasons, some easy to solve, some impossible. Abortion has the appeal of smashing all the problems at once, wiping the slate clean. It is brutal in its efficiency, though; the solutions are roughly yanked out through the woman's aching heart. Her right to abort is noisily and publicly celebrated; her long years of pondering the cost are more privately endured. Abortion is forever.

The pregnancy care center offers a patchwork quilt of help that is thin in many places—not enough housing, not enough car seats, not enough medical care. Too often the deepest problem is one beyond the mending of any stranger's kindness: the woman's need for the baby's father to love and cherish her, to give her the protection and provision that the center, a poor substitute, scrambles to supply. But what the center can give is encouragement, the strength of sisterhood, the strength of other women who know what it's like and who won't let you down. When hope mends the quilt, sometimes it is enough.

Marilyn puffs, squints through the smoke to line up her pills. She's got twenty years of not letting you down. When a heart attack landed her in the hospital last year, her co-laborers would get furtive, whispered phone calls at moments seized when the doctor and her husband were out of earshot. Now she's back running the Auburn Center, a toll-free hotline that crosses Maryland and unites its nearly fifty storefront pregnancy care centers. Women phoning in are given information about help available at their nearest center, plus plenty of kind words and reassurance on the spot. Each call is logged, and tagged as belonging to one of twenty request categories, with 2300–2800 calls received each month.

The Auburn Center's phones are staffed "in the garage—I mean the annex" behind Catonsville's Pregnancy Center West. A staffer answers calls from 9:00 AM till 11:30 PM with short breaks; at other times a service answers which pages Marilyn or her daughter Barbie, and can patch them in with a frightened girl unwilling to leave her number. And Barbie isn't the only other Szewczyk in the field. Marilyn rattles off a list of other kids and their spouses—Lynnie, Ann, Andy, Cathy, Richard—plus her own mother, Kathryn, who answer phones, fold baby clothes, and keep the computer humming. When Marilyn began the hotline in 1982, she originally staffed it by asking friends and relatives, "How much money do you need me to pay you for you to quit your job and do this?" The answer was in the range of $400 a month ("and it's still about the same," she chuckles).

Marilyn's co-worker Anne arrives as I ask about difficult calls. Anne says she just returned a call to the man who had phoned to confess that he was having sex with his daughter. He had asked for help; Anne called back with lists of resources and phone numbers. "He kept going 'Uh-huh,' but I could tell he wasn't writing it down," she says, dejected. Hotline work is frustrating: no eye contact, no way to know what the caller decides to do. Marilyn describes the call from a 13-year-old black girl who was afraid she was pregnant. "I said, 'Listen, honey, even if you're not pregnant, you have got to stop doing this.' The girl said, 'I do?' like she was completely surprised. I said, 'Yes, you don't have to do this.' 'I don't?' She didn't seem to know it was OK not to have sex."

Do people abuse the toll-free number? Rude or obscene calls? Marilyn and Anne, who have seen it all, laugh. "We had one young boy from Frederick who called every day. We were able to find out who he was. So the next time he called, I said, 'Now listen, Allen . . .' He hung up and never called again!"

MARILYN'S OFFICE IS A CHEERFUL little square building that bears no resemblance to a garage. Inside it is crammed with desks, books, videotapes, audiotapes, posters, fax, phones, and a monster copier. She sits at her desk rolling off anecdotes, pausing each few minutes to answer the phone. When the phone rings, she turns her back on me and covers the phone like a mother hen; her voice drops and becomes confidential and gentle.

Right now she is annoyed with one of the centers in her phone network. A woman had called after her husband suddenly walked out; she had children three, two, and one, plus fourteen-week-old twins. She had no money, and no diapers or formula; for the last few days she had been feeding the twins sugar water. Dependent on public transportation, she had been making rounds at public assistance offices, with the three-year-old carrying one of the twins.

Marilyn referred the woman to her nearest center—but they told her that she would have to produce a birth certificate and other documentation before they would help her. "Can you imagine it?" Marilyn asks, angry and amused at the same time. "They're afraid someone will take advantage of them. Who cares? I'd be afraid that someone who really needs my help would get by. I don't care if some people take advantage. I'm not going to miss *your* baby." Her finger jabs for emphasis.

When the woman called back, Marilyn took it on herself to help. She bought a carload of groceries and took some baby furniture, clothes, toys, and set out to find the section of Baltimore called Westport. "It's near Cherry Hill—you know, that's always on the news for another shooting?" When she stopped to ask directions at a gas station, the black attendant pleaded with her, "Lady, you don't want to go there! *We* don't even go there!" But Marilyn and Barbie found the place: past overflowing dumpsters and abandoned cars, "But inside it was neat and clean as a pin, with nice furniture, not expensive but nice. How she keeps it that clean with five little kids I don't know. I have three grandchildren living with me, and I know my house doesn't look that good!"

NORTH AND WEST FROM BALTIMORE the hills begin to roll, lapping up at the base of the Appalachian Mountains, with farmland, woods, and vacant businesses dotting the route. Just before the Pennsylvania border lies Taneytown, founded in 1754, a cluster of worn brick buildings with white wooden porches, glowing rose today under a drizzly pearl sky. Taneytown was the home of Supreme Court Chief Justice Roger Taney, whose infamous *Dred Scott* decision (1857) decreed that blacks were not citizens; many have suggested a parallel to *Roe v. Wade*'s denial of personhood to the unborn.

Marilyn's daughter-in-law Gloria has set up the Carroll County Pregnancy Center right at the town's crossroads. Her building is one room wide, going back deep into the block. The front section is the "Bear-ly Used Boutique," the town's thrift shop, with an extra-large rack of maternity clothes. Prices are posted, but are negotiable down to free. The next room back is a waiting room/lounge shared by clients and volunteers; then comes the computer room, pregnancy testing room, a large closet where layettes are stored, and an inviting counseling room in apricot and blue with a well-cushioned couch and a pillowed rocker. Tucked around the L by the back door is Gloria's "office"—a cluttered desk.

Gloria is a willowy blond with large, limpid eyes. She explains that the thrift shop is a unique feature for a pregnancy center; it was begun as a source of funds and has become a mission in its own right. "It gives some dignity back to the young girls who come here—they can pick out the clothes they like."

Dignity is important to the families, mostly white, mostly farming, that live around here. The area is economically depressed, and many businesses have closed. But, as Marilyn had said, "They're too proud to admit that they're hungry." She had described how Gloria has had to buy up a load of groceries and go to a client's house with a white lie: "Somebody gave me all this food, and I have to give it away or it will just go bad! Can you take some?"

Gloria says that her average client is an eighteen-year-old girl in a steady relationship with a boy she plans eventually to marry. What they didn't plan was for pregnancy to complicate the picture. "They're naive, following the trend for teen sex, and have an unrealistic idea that they can have sex and everything will be fine."

Gloria describes a case where the girl came in with the boy, plus both mothers. She giggles a bit at the memory; the mothers were furious with each other, fighting over the kids' heads and volleying the blame back and forth. Gloria took the girl aside for a long talk about abstinence, while the mother listened in. "But I've been saying those same things for years!" she exclaimed. Gloria sits back. "Sometimes they'll hear it from me, where the parents were never able to get through."

The center's funding is cobbled together from many sources. In 1992 the Boutique brought in $4,363 as clear profit; it is staffed by volunteers and sells donated goods, so it has no expenses (rent and utilities are covered by the pregnancy center). Another $11,800 was raised in various ways: a ham raffled at Easter raised $500, and the annual Walkathon brought in nearly $3,000. The Walkathon is a fixture of pregnancy center fundraising across the country, probably the most popular money-making tool. In Taneytown, about a hundred walkers signed up supporters to donate so much per mile to the center. On a sunny Saturday, pushing strollers and wearing T-shirts with the center's name, the walkers followed the designated route in a festive throng, and later collected the pledged donations. In past years, volunteers have delivered business lunches to raise funds, canvassing area offices and taking orders for homemade sub sandwiches. Gloria says she also has two churches that give regularly, and a number of individuals give $5–25 per month. In 1992 she served 392 clients.

During the last ten minutes an incessant "Mrow? Mrow? Mrow?" has struck up outside the back door. Gloria opens the door, and in walks a very tall, very thin cat: on an oversized frame designed to carry twenty pounds of burly catflesh is stretched about eight pounds of hungry orange kitty. Gloria gives him a skeptical look as he begins pounding his head against her ankles, purring like a furnace. "Mr. Bones. He belongs to the people upstairs, but I don't think they feed him," she confides. "We've sort of adopted him, but I keep his food out on the back porch." Gloria, like all those in her line of work, is constantly making decisions about what kind of help helps and what kind of help ultimately hurts. I ask how she keeps clients from becoming over-dependent. She considers this question with an air of regret.

"We took a hard look at our files awhile back and realized that we were enabling some people to use us. If they ran out of money at the end of the month, they'd call us—we've paid electric, fuel, given diapers," she said. "We decided that, once we'd helped people three times, we would require them to get involved with the services the county offers, teaching budget planning, job training, and so forth. Obviously those sort of skills are not there. If somebody has $20, but they decide to spend it on cigarettes, well, we're not going to support that decision."

Gloria is looking to move to bigger quarters. At the edge of town stands a big house on a hill, and she imagines using every corner: the clothes closet will fill the basement; a Christian book and gift store on the main floor; pregnancy care services on the second floor, and on the third floor two bedrooms for emergency housing ("Sometimes we need up to thirty days to get a client into services"). The owner, she thinks, would rather sell to a ministry like hers than have the house torn down for a commercial building. The mortgage is not prohibitive, but she has to raise $25,000 for the down payment. She's writing letters to friends.

I am thinking about Gloria's instinctive, practical generosity. I am imagining that, the next time she goes to put food out on the back porch for Mr. Bones, someone in a limo puts a paper bag holding $25,000 on the front porch for her.

I ask how she got into this line of work, and she laughs and shakes her head. "Marilyn is just relentless! Every gathering always turns back to a discussion of the issues." She smiles as she recalls. "When we lived closer to Baltimore, I volunteered at the center there, but when we moved way out here I thought, 'Thank goodness, I've gotten away from all that!' There's no abortion in Carroll County. But soon after I got here a neighbor's child called up; she said a friend was pregnant and wanted her to drive her to Hagerstown for an abortion. I hated to admit it, but I realized that we needed a pregnancy center. I told Marilyn, and do you know what she did?" Gloria's really laughing now. "She gave me a grocery bag—just a plain, plastic grocery bag—with about thirty pieces of literature in it, and a check for $50. And she said, 'Go open a pregnancy center.'" She shakes her head at the memory. "How did I get into this line of work? From just being stupid and not knowing that I should not listen to Marilyn."

"Nobody warned me that I should not listen to Marilyn," she laughs.

HEADING SOUTH out of Baltimore, almost to Washington, DC, you will arrive at the oldest pregnancy care center in Maryland, the Pregnancy Aid Center in College Park. The Center occupies a rambling, two-story, turn-of-the-century house, whose antique charms are now encased in sheet paneling, drop acoustical tile ceilings, and mustard-yellow aluminum siding. The center was founded nineteen years ago, director Mary Jelacic tells me, "by a group of students at the University of Maryland who were incensed about *Roe v. Wade*; they asked, 'Why isn't anyone addressing the needs of women in crisis pregnancy?' They set up a counseling center that's been operating ever since."

Unexpected pregnancies became even more of a crisis in 1988, when local hospitals cut back the number of charity patients they would accept. But the Pregnancy Aid Center was ready, having developed facilities for on-site prenatal care. In addition to the usual pregnancy center offerings of practical and emotional support, clients could come to the Center's clinic for a medical exam and be assured that they and their babies were progressing toward a healthy birth. Patients are asked to give $5 per visit, but the fee is waived whenever necessary.

Mary Jelacic believes that the center's ability to offer medical care is what makes the difference between choosing abortion and choosing birth for many of these women. The clientele is 85% Hispanic, and their choices are often limited by language, finances, and legal status. While they can make room for a new child, the up-front charge of thousands of dollars for the delivery is daunting. The Pregnancy Aid Center fills the gap, allowing immigrant Hispanic women the same choices that their more wealthy, insured American sisters enjoy.

Ideological partisanship does not stand in the way of serving women. Three of the doctors who previously staffed the clinic labeled themselves pro-choice; they believed that birth was a choice that should also be available and supported with quality care. These three have now all moved from the area, and certified nurse-midwives from the faculty of Georgetown University's School of Midwifery have taken their place. Michaela Donohue and Becky Skovgaard will be seeing patients today.

The Pregnancy Aid Center's client load—2,000 per year, 800 using medical services—makes use of every square foot of space. An assortment of high chairs, squeezed out of interior storage, stand in a forlorn group outside the front door, as if hoping to be let back in. Just inside there is a sunny waiting room with six mostly-mismatched chairs and a sofa; in the next room, the office, there is a metal desk and another seven chairs. Boxes are stuffed under chairs and stacked in corners.

Notices and signs tacked to the walls are in Spanish and English, or sometimes only Spanish ("Consulta Legal Gratuita"), and pamphlets with titles like "Esta mi bebe tomando suficiente leche?" line the wall rack. Further down the hall are rooms for counseling and storage of clothing, and Mary's office in a large and utterly crammed space that was once no doubt a parlor. Now a large copier sits in the bay window. Upstairs there are two examining rooms, more storage, and another large waiting room with a doctor's scale and specimen cups.

Waiting in the office this lunchtime are two Hispanic women and a blonde with two children; an African woman wrapped in bright batik represents another segment of the Center's clientele. The blonde has completed her examination, and is telling her kids that it turns out the early contractions are nothing to worry about, she's having them because "I'm on my feet with the band so much." The girl, about 10, runs over to the fetal models and brings back the one of six-month size. "The midwife said that the baby is about this size now." She shows it to her mother, a pink doll the size of her hand, curled in on itself and sucking a thumb. The mother gazes at it and beams a dreamy smile; sister and brother frown at the rival with a bit more ambivalence.

I am invited to the upstairs waiting room where the staff is having lunch. Here the Wide World of Chairs theme is continued. Mary Jelacic is a bright-eyed brunette in a red cotton dress and a ponytail. Decades in America have not erased her Scottish accent (the Croatian surname comes from her husband). She came to the Center as director in 1981, when she read in her church bulletin an offer of part-time employment. Her children were in school and it seemed a good time to take on something not overly demanding (or so it appeared at the time). Mary's training was in Special Education, and she says, "I considered unplanned pregnancy to be a somewhat handicapping condition."

Also lunching with us are Alicia, a new volunteer, a man named Terry (whom Mary jokingly refers to as "el jefito"), and midwife Michaela Donohue; soon the second midwife, Becky Skovgaard, joins us. Everyone is downing sloppy sub sandwiches, and Terry jokes about raiding the layette closet for bibs.

How does the Center find funds to operate? Michaela says wryly, "Mary goes out on the streets and begs." Mary laughs and explains that the Center is listed with the Combined Federal Campaign, and can be designated through United Way. There are also individual and church contributions, plus grants from the March of Dimes, the Giant Food grocery chain, the Knights of Columbus, the Knights of Malta, the Archdiocese of Washington, and a few local foundations.

How busy does it get? Mary recounts the story of the infamous evening, a couple of years ago, when they had thirty-three patients come to the clinic. The doctor attending that evening was there for the first time, on loan from Holy Cross Hospital; his specialty was infertility. ("He didn't find much of that here," someone comments.) It was a chaotic time: "Number thirteen was an ectopic—that set him back a wee bit," and she was rushed off to the hospital. Apparently the doctor had expected to finish at a reasonable hour, and had to keep making trips to the phone to cancel dates and appointments. Finally he got to number 32, who had been sitting quietly on the steps all evening with her hands folded on top of her belly. But once she got on the table, the doctor yelled, "Mary! Th' feet are in the cervix!" This baby was about to come into the world wrong-way-around, and such a case usually requires an emergency Cesarean. Mary called the Fire and Rescue Department located across the street, which made the short trip sirens blazing and arrived before the patient had managed to get back into her clothes. She was hastily dressed and sent off to the hospital with her chart pinned to her chest "because she didn't speak any English, you know."

Only when the Keystone Kops frenzy had died down did they realize that the last patient, number 33, had been sitting patiently in the back room with her clothes off all that time. As she took her leave, the doctor told Mary, "You took ten years off my life tonight!" He never returned. The next day Sister Jane Anne at Holy Cross Hospital scolded Mary: "What did you do to our boy!" The doctor moved out of state and into the relative calm of an infertility practice. Mary winds up the story by talking about that breech baby: his name is Mario and he's now two-and-a-half. Every year the mother brings Mary a potted plant and a birthday party invitation; every year Mary goes.

We are interrupted by a Hispanic boy of about 15 with headphones slung around his neck and a heart-melting bashful smile. He is the son of a patient, and he asks to speak to Mary; he wants to know if he can become a volunteer at the center. When Mary returns, discussion ensues about this boy, who they are afraid is becoming a "parental child"—he is missing school in order to take care of his mother and siblings. The room becomes an extended-family conference on the boy's welfare and family situation.

As I watch them I am thinking about how much Mary does for women and their families. I picture Marilyn driving into Westport with a carload of gifts, and Gloria cocking an eye at the wildly purring Mr. Bones. I am thinking about the charge that pro-lifers only care about fetuses. I haven't heard any of them talk about a fetus yet.

Instead, Mary and Michaela and the others talk about the Center's clients, most of whom are between the ages of 12 and 25. Just over 50% turn out not to be pregnant; like Gloria, Mary encourages abstinence for young women: "They're adolescent, their bodies are still growing, they're not in stable relationships—abstinence is best." She says that many feel that sexual activity is almost a requirement; if everyone is telling you to use condoms, you can't use them without having sex. Some just need permission to stop.

Mary encourages teens, most of all, to talk to their parents. Yes, she agrees, when your parents find out you're pregnant they'll hit the roof. But if you have a secret abortion and get injured (like a 16-year-old girl in this county who died after having a legal abortion without her parent's knowledge), your parents will find out anyway, and then they'll have three shocks to endure: My child was sexually active, got pregnant, and had an abortion! Mary urges, "Tell them first."

To make this easier, Mary or volunteers will go with the child to tell the parents. They do this at the Center or the home, or meet them at McDonald's. About a third of the time, the client chooses abortion. Some of these come back for medical care or post-abortion counseling; the Center does not reject or condemn.

Like Gloria, Mary is hoping to move her Center to a new building. Her Scots blood makes her tenacious in a bargain; when the center was evicted from the present building years ago, she didn't leave ("We had no place to go, so we stayed") and instead got an interest-free loan and bought the building. She laughs, "The board thought it was time to fire me because they thought I'd lost me marbles." Now she has her eye on the new medical building down the street. The price is dropping fast, but she's patient enough to wait, and then there's the matter of an absence of funds to purchase it. But she believes the building is for her. It will put her a block from the local abortion clinic.

As I leave, Mary is speaking earnestly to a Hispanic client, working hard to assemble sentences in Scottish-accented Spanish. Here we have a Scot with a Croatian name speaking Spanish to a woman from El Salvador, while upstairs women with Scandinavian and Irish backgrounds are examining pregnant women from Mexico and Cameroon. All around the world, women make babies and have babies the same way. And all around the world, other women help and support them. This is how they do it in College Park, Maryland.

WHO WOULD OPPOSE THE WORK of centers like these? They don't threaten anyone's access to abortion, but just offer support to those who make a different choice. Without the thousands of pregnancy centers like these giving hope and help across the country, the abortion rate would be much higher than its present four thousand per day. Pregnancy care centers give women an alternative to abortion.

But that is precisely the problem. Abortion clinics must be equipped and operated every day, by professionals who are less likely to be willing to work for a sandwich and a smile. Expenses roll up continuously, and aren't paid by women who choose life.

Consider, for example, Planned Parenthood Federation of America, with a hundred affiliates offering abortion—thirty of those doing abortions through the second trimester (that is, until the seventh month), when it is a grisly procedure indeed. These hundred clinics constitute the largest chain of abortion outlets in America. While Planned Parenthood insists that their counseling helps pregnant women fully understand their alternatives, past clients frequently say that it was directed toward helping them fully understand that continuing the pregnancy would be a disaster.

American Life League, a pro-life advocacy group, reports that a review of "yearly projection for early abortion counseling" at two Planned Parenthood referral facilities in California reveals that 98% of women at one clinic and 93% at the other "chose" abortion. Jim Sedlak's watchdog group, STOPP, reports that internal documents for some Planned Parenthood clinics show the projected number of abortions the clinic expects that year. "Any increase of actual over projections is reported as a 'gain,'" writes Sedlak. "Any decrease is reported as a 'loss.'"

While it seems a bit harsh to designate the choice to give birth as a "loss," that is not to say that those who provide abortion are motivated only by money. The woman with an unplanned pregnancy stands between two camps, each of which offers her their own brand of compassion. Those who offer abortion can rightly say that it is a quick way to solve many problems at once and send the woman on her way. If pregnancy is the problem, get rid of the pregnancy.

Those who provide alternatives to abortion believe that pregnancy is just one facet of the woman's larger and more complex life. They believe she is not best served by treating her as merely a polluted uterus in need of a good scrubbing. Her life is tangled with the life of her child growing within, woven with the lives of the child's father, with her own parents, friends, and coworkers in a tapestry of lives. To remove the child is to cut a hole in the tapestry, by literally cutting into human flesh, tearing the child apart and tearing the mother's heart. Unplanned pregnancy is not one problem, but a host of problems, great and small; pregnancy care providers try to solve them, one at a time.

Problem pregnancy is associated frequently with poverty, and Planned Parenthood selects the poorer neighborhoods; it is popularly believed that abortion is the best solution for the poor. At any rate, this belief is popular with those who are not poor. Polls regularly show that those with higher income levels are the most likely to endorse public funding of abortion, a gift that the recipients are not eager to accept. David Gergen, in an editorial written before he joined the Clinton administration, pointed out that a 1992 *Reader's Digest* poll discovered "poorer Americans are the most opposed to federal funding [for abortion]. Among those earning less than $15,000 per year, opposition ran 63 to 32 percent against funding, while those making over $60,000 favored it by 57 to 41 percent." Gergen asks, "Is Clinton listening to the people he wants to help?"

When people offer to help you by giving you money to eliminate your children, there's an implied message that's hard to miss. A friend who worked in an abortion referral center stocked a flyer which explained how we could reduce our tax burden by helping poor women have abortions; one day a Hispanic client came in, slapped the flyer on the counter, and hissed, "This is what you *really* think of us." Margaret Sanger, the founder of Planned Parenthood, was an enthusiastic eugenicist who wanted "to create a race of thoroughbreds" by rectifying "the unbalance between the birth rate of the 'unfit' and the 'fit.'" Planned Parenthood still has great admiration for Sanger, and president Faye Wattleton said a few years ago that the organization is "just following in the footsteps" of its founder.

Two brands of compassion, each offering what they think is best, but one gets the lion's share of funding. While pregnancy care centers are a woman-to-woman operation, with funds raised in batches through bake sales and small grants, abortion is more lavishly supported from above. Planned Parenthood Federation of America is the recipient of impressive grants from a long list of foundations and corporations, from Helena Rubenstein to the Pew Charitable Trusts to the New York Times Company. In a typical year, $125 million was received via government grants and contracts. Planned Parenthood has fought for federal funding of abortion, and with the expanded provisions of the Hyde Amendment will now be able to charge more abortions to the public purse. Some states, as well, use taxpayer funds to underwrite abortions: in Maryland the bill totals $3 million per year. There is plenty of money from above to eliminate the children of the poor, and little need for bake-sale fundraising from below. The director of Planned Parenthood in Maryland is a well-mannered, sober Bostonian in a dark suit; it is hard to imagine him raising funds by poking his head in an office door, like Gloria's volunteers, and asking how many want a pastrami sub.

But even without lush funding, pregnancy care centers will go on. The abortion battle may be most loudly fought in the political arena, but few pregnant women are found there. Where women in need go, other women go to help, in Taneytown and College Park and three thousand other centers across the land. It is a subversive work, when women help women give birth, and it is the best proof yet of the power of sisterhood.

8 | FEMINISM'S NEXT GENERATION

MY TEENAGED DAUGHTER and I were out on an errand, and as we drove we listened to one of her favorite female artists. Ani DiFranco is the kind of guitarist who leaves you slack-jawed; her command of the instrument is complete, with trills and intricate picking running up and down the scale. Her voice is an acquired taste, I suppose—acrobatic and tightly controlled, but with rather a sharp edge. She sounds like a housecat after a couple of espressos. I'm impressed by DiFranco's gifts, but as I said to Megan, "I wouldn't want to be in a small room with her, much less an elevator."

"Oh, this is one of my favorites," Megan said, as the chords of a new song began. "It's so typical of her. She's just saying, 'I'm a woman, and I'm playing a guitar!'"

Megan smiled tranquilly as DiFranco elbowed her way aggressively into another song, this one about being a woman in a man's business but nevertheless succeeding. It had a defiant edge. My daughter has an easygoing nature and can view the performer's somewhat frantic style with detached amusement. But listening to the lyrics cast me back a couple of dozen years.

When this performer was a baby, or not even yet imagined by anyone but God, I was a cranky feminist college student. I thrived on anger. The central fact of existence for me was that life was unfair to women, that men got all the breaks and we got cheated, and that we had to be courageous and defiant. We prided ourselves on being "uppity women." Sassiness was a virtue.

I found that the further I got into it, the more mesmerizing this formula became. It resolved any number of ambivalent questions with a simple flip: all problems are the fault of men, we're small and oppressed but spunky, so everything we do is right. We had cast ourselves in an irresistible cinematic role, that of brazen young hero. We ran on the most durable fuel known to humankind, that of (self-)righteous indignation.

DiFranco's music comes to me across a time warp: twenty-five years later, it's the same old song. It's frightening in retrospect to see how stubbornly durable that anger and that hip-young-hero self-image are. The record skips, and we repeat the same line over and over again: we're wronged, we're right, we're noble, fierce, and cool. Has there really been no progress in all these years? Are women still really at the same point of wicked oppression?

Young women, particularly young Christian women, look at contemporary feminism with understandable puzzlement. It is true that, some twenty or thirty years ago, women were not expected to be capable of succeeding in typically male professions. It's true that they were dismissed as fluff-heads, "woman drivers," charming incompetents. It is further true that the determination of many strong and talented women has reversed that stereotype, and now being a woman is frequently an asset, for tokenist reasons if nothing else.

On the other hand, some things have gotten worse. The expectation that women would place that forbidden and hard-won career ahead of children and family turned out to be a disaster. But you can only deny biology so long; now the fastest-growing type of household is the housewife-workadaddy model, with younger couples taking the lead. Young moms state their determination to raise their own children; they and their husbands know from experience what it's like to have a mom who placed career first, and they want no part of it.

The sexual revolution, likewise, was a disaster for women. For women sex is connected with love, love with commitment, commitment with marriage, and all this with the stability necessary for raising a child. Anything that lessens the pressures on men to be faithful to women, to support them and fulfill their family obligations, hurts women in the long run. In areas like these, women have far to go before they achieve the kind of social changes they need.

Though much has changed since I was a young feminist, one thing has not: the tone of the DiFranco song, identical to the song of my youth. This peculiar psychodrama of feminism, thriving on a sense of being wronged and being nobly defiant, is its own poison. It's an incantation that subtly distorts the whole world—and places the singer firmly at the center. This is dangerous to the soul.

In advising young women about feminism, I would say, listen carefully to what women's real needs are. If you imagine a composite of all women, of all ages, from all over the world and through all time, the central fact of shared existence would be childrearing. So women need, more than anything else, faithful men. Some aspects of contemporary feminism may be aimed at that goal; some may not. It's not a matter of swallowing either feminism or antifeminism whole; you can pick and choose.

But there is one caution I would offer: don't call yourself a feminist. There's something wrong with the very term, the very identity—something wrong with identifying yourself as over-against someone else (men, the establishment, the "bad guys"). The term "feminism" unnecessarily divides the world into competing teams, into those who supposedly have power and those who do not.

The old familiar song heard fresh on the DiFranco album gives a warning. This noble, suffering self-image is so seductive that it can change the very way you view the world. It is a tasty lie. And as pleasant as it is, it's utterly unproductive. If it had done some good, the song would have changed in twenty-five years, or would at least now sound dated. But, no, the rage is as fresh today as it was long ago. It's only circular rage. It doesn't go anywhere.

Long ago I realized that being a feminist was doing something to me, something bad. I was angry all the time and, worse, taking a perverse pleasure in being angry. I was becoming contemptuous and sour. My view of reality was being distorted. For this reason, I pulled back from my feminist connections and weaned myself from some of the more noxious reading and activities. I didn't disagree with feminism's goals at that point, but I knew that, in practice, it was destroying me.

What I hear of DiFranco's rage could have been lifted intact from my life long ago. She is a gifted performer, and I understand why my daughter enjoys her work; I can enjoy much of it myself. But this particular strand of her message looms toward me out of a dark mirror of history. I can understand how appealing it is, how nearly compelling, how strong and true it rings. And I know that it is poison.

9 | THE WOMEN OF DISNEY

IN THE MIDDLE OF MY LIFE'S JOURNEY I came to myself, alone in a dark plastic poncho at the Haircuttery.

It was a few days after my forty-third birthday, and I had not received a Cinderella watch packaged in a tiny clear-plastic glass slipper. For awhile there I received one every birthday, because I kept losing them. That was some years ago. At that time I intended to be a grownup lady one day, and wear a crown and a long fancy dress. Everything about me would get bigger, except my feet; these would get smaller and smaller until they were the same size as Cinderella's, and I could wear her tiny shoes. I think I kept losing the watches in secret hope of collecting two shoes and making a pair. However, I kept losing the shoes too, so my plans were dashed.

In the middle of my life's journey I see in the big black-framed mirror a grownup lady getting an E-Z Kare haircut, wearing E-Z Kare clothes, which conceal an E-Z Kare figure. I had forgotten my plan to be Cinderella about now, and at this point it's probably too much trouble.

Like an army of other little girls over several generations, my idea of female loveliness was shaped by the women of Disney. I imagine that cohort resembling the star-stables maintained by the

big movie studios of the thirties: glamorous women lunching os-
tentatiously together, sipping champagne, flipping cigarette ashes
in each other's feather boas.

The Disney women, ageless, still meet covertly in a private club
overlooking the Pacific. The waves crash on the rocks below, and
they lift toasts in their little three-fingered hands. To us. We taught
a million little girls what womanhood is like. Too bad none of them
could make it. Then they snicker.

With these thoughts in mind I sat down with my teenaged
daughter, Megan, to review the oeuvre produced by these women
over the years. The first full-length Disney animation film was *Snow
White*, released in 1937. Such an extended stretch of animation, a
particularly labor-intensive form of filmmaking, had never been con-
templated before. A thank-you note from Walt to his crew is in-
serted in the opening credits.

Snow White concerns a princess compelled to dress in rags and
scrub the floor by a jealous, wicked stepmother. If you're taking
notes, it might be a good idea to jot that down, because when the
motif pops up again you can check it off. She is, to all appearances,
killed by her nemesis, but comes to life again at "Love's First Kiss."
Make a note of that, too.

But though the story gets recycled, the ladies change dramatically. Snow White is a plump little thing with a tiny, trilling voice
that makes you want to swat at mosquitoes. Her lips are red as a
rose, hair black as ebony, and skin white as snow; says so right here.
She has a round chubby face with wide-set eyes, no jaw line, no
nose—just dots for nostrils. Her eyes may not be bigger than her
stomach, but they're bigger than her mouth, which is the minute
red embouchure of Betty Boop. In fact, 1937 is late for this standard of beauty; she's a 1920s babydoll, showing plenty of chest but
no décolletage, giggling and shooing critters with her plump little

arms. Give her a few drinks and she'd turn into an IT girl to rival Clara Bow.

I checked with Megan for lessons learned about ideal womanhood from Snow White. "I always wished animals would follow me around," she said, "but I wasn't pretty enough."

This is a scary movie, I mean a *really* scary movie. These early feature-length animations weren't intended primarily as children's films. When the wicked queen chortles that Snow White will be "Buried alive!" and kicks a water jug crashing into a prisoner's skeleton, it seems small comfort that she couldn't even change her clothes without using a magic potion.

The next in our series is *Cinderella* (1950), which concerns a princess compelled to dress in rags and scrub floors by a jealous, wicked stepmother (did you check it off?). But what a difference in girls. "That's a grownup voice!" said Megan, and indeed it is; Cinderella may not be all-the-way grownup, but she's the sturdy, blooming ideal of postwar womanhood just the same. She has a nose, a normal-sized mouth, and wavy honey-colored hair just past her shoulders. She's got the simple goodness of the young Donna Reed, till she gets wrapped in that fabulous white ball gown and, with upswept hair, turns into Grace Kelly.

Cinderella offers a plus for the clinical observer: a chance to see what ugly princesses would look like. Drusilla and Anastasia have jug ears, thin lips, and strange noses that combine a ski-slope top with a bulbous undercarriage. Avoid looking like this, is the subliminal message. You can also compare older women. The wicked stepmother has maintained a taut wasp-waisted figure, magnificent posture, and a grand rise of gray hair striped with a blaze of white. The fairy godmother has a kindly smile, multiple chins, white hair, and the figure of an old pillow. She's tremendously appealing, and sings a great song, "Bibbidi-Bobbidi-Boo."

A mere nine years later, production quality had slid steeply down-hill. *Sleeping Beauty* (1959) opens with a parade sequence in which flattened figures seem to be sliding past each other on parallel tracks. Even the lyrics of the parade-scene song consist of little more than "All hail the Princess Aurora," over and over; I imagine the lyricist was at deadline and panicking. Aurora is doomed to prick her finger and sleep until "True Love's Kiss" awakens her (check it off).

The Princess Aurora, a.k.a. Briar Rose, a.k.a. Sleeping Beauty, seems even older than Cinderella, although the action is supposed to take place on the eve of her sixteenth birthday. "She could be thirty!" Megan says. She could be Barbie, too, that other paragon of loveliness who made her debut in 1959. Like Barbie, Aurora has a tiny waist and a large bosom; unlike the '59 Barbie, she has an avalanche of curling yellow hair that tumbles to her waist. Barbie did not achieve such a mane until her accurately named incarnation of the mid-eighties, "Totally Hair Barbie."

There's a subtle change in Aurora's personality, compared with previous princesses. She's more assertive, more intense; in some shots she looks almost fierce. Presenting women who are strong but not smart-alecky is a continuing problem for Disney from here on. On the other hand, an earlier problem is resolved: when the Handsome Prince showed up, everything would get boring. Both the previous films ended within minutes of the rescue. *Sleeping Beauty* has a fuller plot, better characterizations, and a role for the Handsome Prince that makes him more than a Ken doll—more than Ken himself, likewise making his wooden debut in 1959, could say.

There is, inexplicably, a thirty-year gap before the princesses return. Disney feature animation during this time covered mostly boy and adventure themes (*The Jungle Book, The Sword in the Stone*); I am at a loss to explain why. The closest to a Disney woman during this time would be Maid Marian, co-star of *Robin Hood* (1973).

She's a fox, I mean a vixen—no, really, the four-legged kind. *Robin Hood* demonstrated an early embrace of diversity by featuring an all-animal cast.

Marian is a princess in a way, a niece of the Crown, but in rebellion against the Establishment. This may be a bow to the hippie ethic of the time. Her foxy-red pelt is more than skin deep; with her paramour, Robin, she is involved in a scheme for the forcible redistribution of wealth. Other than that she's benign enough, with an English accent and a faintly superior quality. She's giddy in love with Robin, and keeps clasping her hands under her chin and exposing four pointy, flesh-shredding teeth. It startled me every time.

Suddenly, at the end of the eighties, we run into a cluster of Disneybabes: Ariel in *The Little Mermaid* (1989), Belle in *Beauty and the Beast* (1991), Jasmine in *Aladdin* (1992), and Pocahontas in the eponymous epic of 1995.

These movies are generally very good. Animation, while not as rounded and shadowed as the early sort, is superior to the flatness of the sixties. In some sequences an astonishing monumentality has been achieved; traveling shots that fly through the mermaid's undersea kingdom or Aladdin's cave are breathtaking to the point of being disorienting. The color is exuberant and supersaturated. The same characters keep recurring, but they're meaty characters; in contrast to the simple lines of the first films, there are lots of subplots and running jokes to keep things bouncing along. The opening sequence of *Beauty and the Beast* is as complex and elaborate as the opening number of Broadway's *Les Misérables*.

That doesn't mean the princesses are more attractive, however. Megan and I disagree as to which is more annoying, Ariel or Belle. Ariel is a feisty little redhead who defies her daddy, hoards shiny trinkets, and smirks. While the other princesses were elaborately draped, Ariel runs around in little more than a clamshell bra and fishtail, looking like jailbait. If she had legs, they'd be in stretch toreador pants. Her belly button is always visible, leading to inconclusive ruminations on just how mer-reproduction is accomplished.

Ariel, at least, looks her age (which she shouts at her daddy: "I'm sixteen!") Aurora's voice at sixteen was mezzo if not alto; she had a knowing quality. Ariel is excitable, headstrong, still a child, and her voice is a clean soprano (not reaching the nosebleed heights of Snow White's, however). She wears a massive burden of red hair. "Her head is too big for her body, and her eyes are too big for her head," says Megan.

I think I dislike this *Little Mermaid* so much because it makes a travesty of the original story. Hans Christian Andersen's mermaid was at the center of a complex drama, sacrificing her life for her beloved even though he marries someone else. The story's refusal to make that innocent bride a villainess is part of what gives it its power; tragedy and nobility meet in exquisite resolution. But Disney's Ariel sabotages the evil false-bride and grabs the prince for herself. It's a story, all right, but it's not the right story.

Megan prefers to loathe Belle. In the opening of *Beauty and the Beast*, Belle is taunted by the village people, who call her "strange but special" because she reads books. Why her bookishness makes her odd is unclear; the purpose seems to be to convince you that the villagers are dolts. Belle is slim and straight, with normal-size chestnut hair in a low ponytail. She's more mature than Ariel, with a more confident manner and lower voice. Belle is the least glamorous of the Disney women.

In a twist, the evil character here is not an older woman but the Ken-doll male lead. Poor Gaston is loaded up with every despicable non-P.C. vice available. In case the little girls aren't getting it, after he talks about hunting (shriek!) and marriage (gasp!) he admonishes Belle, "It's not right for a woman to read. Soon she starts getting ideas and thinking." Gaston is such a straw man he isn't even any fun to hate. Meanwhile, Belle is pouting her impatience with her hometown in song: "There must be more than this provincial life!"

"Both Gaston and Belle think they're better than everyone else," says Megan. "But Belle is smug about it."

Jasmine made her debut in *Aladdin*, a fabulously entertaining movie mostly due to the performance of Robin Williams as the Genie. She's a princess, all right, but something has gone terribly, tragically wrong. Her waist is narrow as a thumb, but her hair is a blooming vast cloud of black, the size of a horse. If this little person were to stand up in real life, the weight of that hair would snap her in the middle like a toothpick. Which would be a completely different kind of movie, one Stephen King might like.

Also, her eyes are too big. Someone told the animators that big eyes make a character appealing, but that's advice to be used judiciously, like "Perfume makes you smell good." The black oval disks in Jasmine's face are the size of turkey platters. They slip past appealing into disturbing, suggesting the fevered dreams of a fetishist.

Mention should be made in passing of Nala, the queen-to-be in *The Lion King* (1994). Nala is a lioness, but the animators were able to prevent what could have been a repeat of the Maid Marian problem by concealing her teeth. One of the refreshing things about Nala is that she's not particularly pretty; she looks good, like a lioness should, without being feminized. Her lips are black and her round ears are right on top of her head, like Mickey's. Belle's edgy feminism is present, but not oppressive: every time Nala wrestles Simba, she pins him.

I was not able to view the most daunting heroine of all, Pocahontas; her video won't be out till spring. Megan, however, has seen her. One day last summer she badgered her two younger brothers

until they agreed to accompany her to the theater for what she promised would be family-fun time. She came home and stood in my
office, grumpy.

"This is Pocahontas," she said. " 'Ooooo! Trees are smart! Wind
has colors! Rocks love you!'"

"This is me," she went on. "'Buh-bye.'"

"This is Pocahontas: 'Ooooo! You wouldn't understand! You're
only an evil whiteskin! You like to kill bunnies!'"

"This is me: 'BUH. BYE.'"

I have seen her Poca-highness in trailers, though. She has the
lantern jaw of a thirties swashbuckler, and the resonant power-voice
of a Broadway musical star. Her eyes are unnaturally wide-set, and
she has no nose, just little dots for nostrils. It's an odd homage:
Snow White had the same attributes. But Snow White ran screaming through the night forest in terror. "Pocahontas wouldn't be running away," Megan observed. "The forest is her friend. She would
be lecturing Snow White." In fact, that's the problem with these
latest princesses, Megan says. You always have the feeling they're
lecturing you.

Although Pocahontas wears a revealing buckskin frock with a
gravity-defying bodice (it's entertaining to imagine what would really happen when it got wet), she's more aggressive, more masculine
than any previous princess. Maybe she's another Disney break-
through: the first cartoon transvestite.

Though I missed the film, Pocahontas is part of my daily life.
Megan found a sticker with her image in a box of cereal and, still
irritated, placed it over the "Start" button on the microwave. Now,
whenever we heat anything, we punch Pocahontas in the nose. It
does yield a quiet satisfaction.

Of all these heroines, it is still Cinderella who, for me, holds the
most appeal. She was unaffected and kind, strong of character with-

out slipping into the annoying smugness of the later Disney women. But it's time to admit that there's little chance I'm going to be able to look like Cinderella. That chance has passed me by, as it passes most little girls.

It's not so hard to let go of a dream when there's another one handy. Though it's probably too late for me to look like Cinderella, I think I can gradually come to look like the fairy godmother. Give me another twenty years. Fluffy, jolly, forgetful, saying things like "mysticaboola"—that should come in handy, since I write for religion magazines a lot. Her voluminous soft lavender robe with no waistline looks a lot more comfortable than Cinderella's party dress. I bet it goes right in the washer-dryer. I picture that lady in the black-framed mirror, and I've got to admit it: finally, the shoe fits.

Handy Clip 'n' Save Reference Card

That woman across the room, so compelling, so strangely familiar. Doesn't she look a little, well, *animated* to you? Could it be one of the Women of Disney, traveling incognito? Before you ask for an autograph and make a fool of yourself, check this handy guide.

If she has . . .	*It could be . . .*
Big Eyes	Jasmine
Big Hair	Jasmine
Big Ears	Nala
Closed Eyes	Aurora
An Attitude	Ariel
Coupla Extra Pounds	Snow White
Pointy Teeth	Maid Marian
Mice	Cinderella
Books	Belle
5:00 Shadow	Pocahontas

10 | THE FLAWS
OF THE FIFTIES

SOME CONSERVATIVE CHRISTIANS are tempted to look back on the 1950s as the golden age. Wouldn't it be great, they think, if families were like the Ozzie-and-Harriet households of that day? Strong two-parent families, where the dads worked and the moms stayed home with the kids. Where kids were cherished and not hurried through childhood. Where "family values" were supported by schools, the media, and entertainment. If only things were like that again . . .

. . . we could raise a new generation of Americans who would take drugs, burn flags, have indiscriminate sex, champion abortion, mock the faith, and complain continuously about what a lousy deal we handed them.

There must have been something wrong with the fifties: they led to the sixties. The kids that grew up in those tidy two-parent homes weren't out of their teens before they began doing all they could to overthrow that wholesome security. We shouldn't try to blindly recapitulate that social experiment before asking: What went wrong?

Though there are many factors, one short response might be: children received *too* much pampering attention. This sounds impossible in an age when millions of children are aborted, abandoned, and institutionalized in faceless day care. But there are two different traditional approaches to childrearing, and they have widely differing results.

In the fifties an attitude toward childhood bloomed which had first sprouted in the Victorian era. In this view, childhood is seen as a carefully delineated, circumscribed experience; it's almost a physical place, a playroom stocked with toys, where precious children linger all a long golden afternoon. Adults look on with wistful, vicarious pleasure, fawning over the tots and shielding them from the harsh winds of the cruel adult world. Adults place a high value on preserving children's "innocence."

But this view expects both too much and too little of children. The assumption of childhood innocence is naive; although children are unknowledgeable about much of the world's evil, they are far from innocent when it comes to the root of inborn sin, self-centeredness. The adult who expects children to be angelic sprites is in for a disappointment. The idea that children are born pure, then gradually corrupted by this evil old world is a Romantic notion of the late eighteenth century; it has no support in Scripture, developmental psychology, or common-sense experience.

The process of unlearning self-centeredness is a difficult, life-long one, elsewhere known as "dying to self." When a child's natural tendency to pamper self goes unchallenged, there's trouble down the road. Witness the late sixties, when my generation took a sledgehammer to every aspect of cozy fifties life we could reach. The Baby Boomer crew is still mirror-gazing in fascination, gluttonous with consumerism, blubbering over its fragile self-esteem. We are a cohort of Emperor Babies, leaving spittle on everything we touch.

But fifties-style childrearing also expected too little of children; it expected them to stay idle children, not adults-in-training. In indulgent childrearing, parents pay attention to children. In the earlier, scriptural approach, children pay attention to parents. Childhood is not a resting-place isolated from the world, but a brisk walk of growing self-discipline and responsibility; at the end, the child has earned the right to be counted as an adult. Childhood is just one phase of a continuum, a path of lifelong growth and accountability before God.

Responsibility parenting does not isolate children in a special protected sphere, but places them at Mom or Dad's knee learning daily the trades, chores, and skills of adulthood. Parents attempt to include their kids in the adult world as much as is feasible. As children accompany a parent moving through the day, they learn, not only skills, but values: how to be courteous, deal fairly, control temper, and plan ahead. If they are not spending those hours watching a parent, they're watching someone else—and learning someone else's values.

An approach that directs attention from child to parent, rather than the reverse, also calls into question another fifties assumption: that a mother's job is full-time doting. Not only did the fifties style of child-centered mothering feed childish self-fascination, but it led to such loneliness, frustration, and depression in some educated women that the feminist movement sprang up in response.

Instead, responsibility mothering includes setting an example of full-fledged adult womanhood. While time spent cuddling and playing on the child's level is an indispensable source of fun and security in a child's life, a mother must also prepare her children for adulthood, not lifelong childhood. Her own long life will encompass many more roles and responsibilities than the intensive child-tending of the early years. So she sets her kids an example of the "virtuous woman" of Proverbs 31, busy with home management, hobbies, and church ministries; she may even keep her hand in a career while caring for small children, by working from home or keeping on top of continuing-education opportunities.

When contemporary Christians look back longingly at the cozy family life of the fifties, we may forget to read the experiment to the end and assess how those kids turned out. Rather than adopting the Ozzie-and-Harriet model wholesale, we should look to older traditions for something more spiritually nutritious.

Jesus used the illustration of a father who, when his son asked for bread, would not give him a stone. In an age when children are treated as property, discarded and killed, we may long to answer the simple call for bread with cuddling and cake. The fifties glow as a time when children were similarly indulged. But the damage those children, now grown, have done will haunt us the rest of our lives. Let's give our children something better than unlimited coddling; let's give them the guidance to grow to mature, responsible lives.

11 | LET'S HAVE MORE TEEN PREGNANCY

TRUE LOVE WAITS. Wait Training. Worth Waiting For. The slogans of teen abstinence programs reveal a basic fact of human nature: teens, sex, and waiting aren't a natural combination. Something there is that does not love a wait.

Over the last fifty years the wait has gotten longer. In 1950, the average first-time bride was just over 20; in 1998 she was five years older, and her husband was pushing 27. If that June groom had launched into puberty at twelve, he'd been waiting more than half his life.

If he *had* been waiting, that is. Sex is the sugar coating on the drive to reproduce, and that drive is nearly overwhelming. It's supposed to be; it's the survival engine of the human race. Fighting it means fighting a basic bodily instinct, akin to fighting thirst.

Yet despite the conflict between liberals and conservatives on nearly every topic available, this is one point on which they firmly agree: young people absolutely must not have children. Though they disagree on means—conservatives advocate abstinence, liberals favor contraception—they shake hands on that common goal. The younger generation must not produce a younger generation.

But teen pregnancy, in itself, is not such a bad thing. By the age of eighteen, a young woman's body is well prepared for childbearing. Young men are equally qualified to do their part. Both may have better success at the enterprise than they would in later years, as some health risks—Cesarean section and Down syndrome, for example—increase with passing years. (The dangers we associate with teen pregnancy, on the other hand, are behavioral, not biological: drug use, STDs, prior abortion, extreme youth, and lack of prenatal care.) A woman's fertility has already begun to decline at 25—one reason the population-control crowd promotes delayed childbearing. Early childbearing also rewards a woman's health with added protection against breast cancer.

Younger moms and dads are likely be more nimble at childrearing as well, less apt to be exhausted by toddlers' perpetual motion, less creaky-in-the-joints when it's time to swing from the monkey bars. I suspect that younger parents will also be more patient with boys-will-be-boys rambunctiousness, and less likely than weary forty-somethings to beg pediatricians for drugs to control supposed pathology. Humans are designed to reproduce in their teens, and they're potentially very good at it. That's why they want to so much.

Teen pregnancy is not the problem. *Unwed* teen pregnancy is the problem. It's childbearing outside marriage that causes all the trouble. Restore an environment that supports younger marriage, and you won't have to fight biology for a decade or more.

Most of us blanch at the thought of our children marrying under the age of 25, much less under 20. The immediate reaction is: "They're too immature." We expect teenagers to be self-centered and impulsive, incapable of shouldering the responsibilities of adulthood. But it wasn't always that way; through much of history, teen marriage and childbearing was the norm. Most of us would find our family trees dotted with many teen marriages.

Of course, those were the days when grown teens were presumed to be truly "young adults." It's hard for us to imagine such a thing today. It's not that young people are inherently incapable of responsibility—history disproves that—but that we no longer expect it. Only a few decades ago, a high school diploma was taken as proof of adulthood, or at least as a promise that the skinny kid holding it was ready to start acting like an adult. Many a boy went from graduation to a world of daily labor that he would not leave until he was gray; many a girl began turning a corner of a small apartment into a nursery. Expectations may have been humble, but they were achievable, and many good families were formed this way.

Hidden in that scenario is an unstated presumption: that a young adult can earn enough to support a family. Over the course of history, the age of marriage has generally been bounded by puberty on the one hand, and the ability to support a family on the other. In good times, folks marry young; when prospects are poor, couples struggle and save toward their wedding day. A culture where men don't marry until 27 would normally feature elements like repeated crop failures or economic depression.

That's not the case in America today. Instead we have an *artificial* situation which causes marriage to be delayed. The age that a man, or woman, can earn a reasonable income has been steadily increasing as education has been dumbed down. The condition of basic employability that used to be demonstrated by a high school diploma now requires a Bachelor's degree, and professional careers that used to be accessible with a Bachelor's now require a Master's degree or more. Years keep passing while kids keep trying to attain the credentials that adult earning requires.

Financial ability isn't our only concern, however; we're convinced that young people are simply incapable of adult responsibility. We expect that they will have poor control of their impulses, be self-centered and emotional, and be incapable of visualizing consequences. (It's odd that kids thought to be too irresponsible for marriage are expected instead to practice heroic abstinence or diligent contraception.) The assumption of teen irresponsibility has broader roots than just our estimation of the nature of adolescence; it involves our very idea of the purpose of childhood.

Until a century or so ago, it was presumed that children were in training to be adults. From early years children helped keep the house or tend the family business or farm, assuming more responsibility each day. By late teens, children were ready to graduate to full adulthood, a status they received as an honor. How early this transition might begin is indicated by the number of traditional religious and social coming-of-age ceremonies that are administered at ages as young as twelve or thirteen.

But we no longer think of children as adults-in-progress. Childhood is no longer a training ground but a playground, and because we love our children and feel nostalgia for our own childhoods, we want them to be able to linger there as long as possible. We cultivate the idea of idyllic, carefree childhood, and as the years for education have stretched, so have the bounds of that playground, so that we expect even "kids" in their mid-to-late twenties to avoid settling down. Again, it's not that people that age *couldn't* be responsible; their ancestors were. It's that anyone, offered a chance to kick back and play, will generally seize the opportunity. If our culture assumed that fifty-year-olds would take a year-long break from responsibility, have all their expenses paid by someone else, spend their time having fun and making forgivable mistakes, our malls would be overrun by middle-aged delinquents.

But don't young marriages tend to end in divorce? If we communicate to young people that we think they're inherently incompetent, that will become a self-fulfilling prophecy, but it was not always the case. In fact, in the days when people married younger, divorce was much rarer. During the last half of the twentieth century, as brides' ages rose from 20 to 25, the divorce rate doubled. The trend toward older, and presumably more mature, couples didn't result in stronger marriages. Marital durability has more to do with the expectations and support of surrounding society than with the partners' ages.

A pattern of late marriage may actually *increase* the rate of divorce. During that initial decade of physical adulthood, young people may not be getting married, but they're still falling in love. They fall in love, and break up, and undergo terrible pain, but find that with time they get over it. They may do this many times. Gradually, they get used to it; they learn that they can give their hearts away, and take them back again; they learn to shield their hearts from access in the first place. They learn to approach a relationship with the goal of getting what they want, and keep their bags packed by the door. By the time they marry, they may have had many opportunities to learn how to walk away from a promise. They've been training for divorce.

As we know too well, a social pattern of delayed marriage doesn't mean delayed sex. In 1950, there were fourteen births per thousand unmarried women; in 1998, the rate had leapt to forty-four. Even that astounding increase doesn't tell the whole story. In 1950 the numbers of births generally corresponded to the numbers of pregnancies, but by 1998 we must add in many more unwed pregnancies that didn't come to birth, but ended in abortion, as roughly one in four of all pregnancies do. My home city of Baltimore wins the blue ribbon for out-of-wedlock childbearing: in 2001, 77% of all births were to unwed mothers.

There are a number of interlocking reasons for this rise in unwed childbearing, but one factor must surely be that when the requirements presumed necessary for marriage rise too high, some

people simply parachute out. Instead of seeing high school gradu-
ates marry at age eighteen, we revert to girls having babies just
past the bar of puberty. Between 1940 and 1998, the rate at which
girls aged ten to fourteen had their first babies almost doubled.
These young moms' sexual experiences are usually classified as "non-
voluntary" or "not wanted." Marriage-before-sex is one way a healthy
culture protects girls.

The idea of returning to an era of young marriage still seems
daunting, for good reason. It is not just a matter of tying the knot
between dreamy-eyed eighteen-year-olds and tossing them out into
the world. Our ancestors were able to marry young because they
were surrounded by a network of support enabling that step. Young
people are not intrinsically incompetent, but they do still have lots
of learning to do, just like newlyweds of any age. In generations
past, a young couple would be surrounded by family and friends
who could guide and support them, not just in navigating the shoals
of new marriage, but also in the practical skills of making a family
work—keeping a budget, repairing a leaky roof, changing a leaky
diaper. It is not good for man to be alone; it's not good for a young
couple to be isolated, either. In this era of extended education, couples
who marry young will likely do so before finishing college, and that
will require practical as well as emotional support from family and
friends.

I got married a week after college graduation, and both my husband and I immediately went to graduate school. We made ends
meet by working as janitors in the evenings, mopping floors and
cleaning toilets. We were far from home, but our church was our
home, and through the kindness of more-experienced families we
had many kinds of support—in fact, all that we needed. When our
first child was born, we were so flooded with diapers, clothes, and
gifts that our only expense was the hospital bill.

Our daughter and older son also married and started families young. Things don't come easy for those who buck the norm, but with the help of family, church, and creative college-to-work programs, both young families are making their way. Early marriage can't happen in a vacuum; it requires support from many directions, and it would be foolish to pretend the costs aren't high.

The rewards are high as well. It is wonderful to see our son and daughter blooming in strong, joyful marriages, and an unexpected joy to count a new daughter and son in our family circle. Our cup overflows with grandchildren as well: come July, we'll have four grandbabies, though the oldest will be barely two. I'll be 49.

It's interesting to think about the future. What if the oldest grandbaby also marries young, and has his first child at the age of 20? I would hold my great-grandchild at 67. There could even follow a great-great-grand at 87. I will go into old age far from lonely. My children and their children would be grown up, available to surround the youngest generation with many resourceful minds and loving hearts. Even more outrageous things are possible: I come from a long-lived family, some of whom went on well past the age of 100. How large a family might I live to see?

Such speculation becomes dizzying—yet these daydreams are not impossible, and surely not unprecedented. Closely looped, mutually supporting generations must have been a common sight in older days when young marriage was affirmed, and young people were allowed to do what comes naturally.

12 | FLOWERS FOR THE FELLAS

IT TOOK ME ABOUT 200 MILES to admit that I was wrong. A few hours back up the road I had been slamming around the house, irritated that I was late leaving on a solo car trip, disorganized, frustrated, and my complaints were gradually enlarging to include anything I could think of regarding my poor husband. I didn't know why it was all his fault, but if you gave me a minute I'd come up with something. Of course, the most glaring crime was that he didn't understand me. Of course, the main reason was that I wasn't making any sense.

A few hundred miles down the road I was feeling, not just personal guilt, but a kind of corporate guilt. It's not just me; a lot of the women I know have this same genius for unreasonableness. In my opinion, you guys deserve some thanks for putting up with us, and some apologies, too.

It took me a few decades to come to that conclusion. Back in my college days, I fiercely held a self-refuting double conviction: first, that men and women are exactly the same; second, that men are jerks and women are perfect. Over the years, married to a guy, raising sons, I learned a few things that modified that opinion. I learned from raising a daughter, too, and having to face some things in that genetic mirror I'd been able to ignore in my own. Here, then, is a long-overdue valentine, some flowers for the fellas.

First, I'm sorry that we get unreasonable like this when we're upset. Your hunch that you can't win in these situations is entirely accurate. It's good of you to stick with us anyway. I don't think I'd go on making lunch dates with a girlfriend who acted that way.

I appreciate that you think you should protect me. That even if you're a total stranger, if someone menaced me chances are you'd automatically come to my aid. Even if it risked your life to do so. I wouldn't do that for you. If you think about it, that's an extraordinary gift for one gender to give another. Just saying "Thanks" doesn't seem enough.

I appreciate that most of the names on the war memorials are male. Even if the armies of the future are as gender-balanced as Noah's ark, that remains a significant fact of history. For centuries men presumed it was their job to die for women; they presumed, in other words, that women's lives are more precious than their own. Take another look at *Saving Private Ryan*: all those extraordinary feats of courage, but not to save Private Ryan's life; he was as expendable as any other private. The real purpose of the mission was to save his mother—not her life, her *feelings*. To men of that time it was obvious that no effort would be too great to spare a mother such terrible grief. For such gallantry I thank you, my grandmother thanks you, and my great-great-great-grandmother thanks you.

I appreciate all the little courtesies that put ladies first. I know that twenty-five years ago I said I'd punch any guy who tried to open a door for me. I was wrong. You meant it in kindness and I was rude not to take it that way.

I think of what life is like in cultures where women are treated as chattel, denied property rights and freedom, where wife-beating is condoned and even expected. Little chivalries and courtesies train men young to treat women gently, and when women mock them we set fire to an insurance policy written strongly in our interest.

I'm sorry for all the harsh jokes about men. A contest in my local paper invited war-of-the-sexes witticisms, and as I read them over I realized that the ones aimed at women were all along the lines of "She sure likes chocolate!" while the ones about men could be summarized, "He's a big boorish idiot!" You might notice a difference there, and once you start noticing it, you see it everywhere. In general, anti-male humor has a bitter, hostile edge lacking in even the dumbest dumb-blonde jokes. Yet guys repeat this banter as much as anyone else; in general, they can roll with self-deprecation a lot better than women can. I think you're very good sports.

Along the same lines, do you notice how many TV ads and sitcoms have this plotline: stupid guy gets his comeuppance from a tough woman? Does anyone ever see any plot that's the reverse? Not on my TV. Again, guys are good sports, good at laughing at themselves, but I think there's a more serious cost to all this hilarity. When all we see are dumb daddies, bad daddies, and absent daddies, there isn't much for a little boy to aspire to. Movie heroes still follow the James Bond convention of carefree, commitment-free womanizing, and images of brave, steadfast family men are few. Yet, despite the lack of appreciation, a lot of men get up and go to work, then come home to their families, every day. We would be wise to celebrate it. This invisible heroism is the backbone of healthy community.

A number of years ago I was having some of these thoughts while driving my two young sons to school. They're different from each other—one is intense, the other tranquil—but even in boyhood both showed some of the classic traits of manliness: strength, patience, gentleness. It was their simple straightforwardness, though, that appeared increasingly sterling to me as their older sister launched into roller-coaster teen years that uncomfortably resembled my own. As I drove, I was feeling guilty that someday they were bound to fall into the hands of women as unreasonable as she and I were. How can a growing boy prepare for that bewildering experience?

"Why is it that guys like girls, anyway?" I asked. "You know, when you grow up you're not going to get candy and flowers from girls who hope you'll like them. When you get engaged, that diamond ring just goes one way. Your wife isn't going to assume it's her job to go downstairs and investigate when there's a noise in the middle of the night. Most people presume that a woman should have the choice of staying home with the kids or going to work, but guys don't get that choice.

"What's more, girls are just *complicated.* Sometimes they get upset and say things they don't even mean, and then get mad at you for not understanding them. Believe me, I know. So why do guys keep liking them?"

The voice of the younger one came piping from the back seat. "Mom!" he exclaimed. "It's 'cause they're babes!"

It's a good thing, too.

13 | WHY HUMANS MATE

GLANCE AROUND ANY ROOM where people are gathered and a curious pattern emerges: they tend to be in pairs. At a church, a concert, a movie theater, a male head is usually near a female head of roughly the same age. Other creatures gather in herds or flocks, or peel off as solitary loners, but humans prefer the couple bond. They gravitate toward it naturally; it's how they seem to want to go through life. Why?

We might as well ask a follow-up question: Why does this pattern fail? Why has our current culture reached such a high level of divorce and dysfunction? Why is there so much pregnancy outside durable bonds, and so much abortion?

To answer these questions we'll have to step back to get a longer view. Step *way* back. Imagine a zookeeper on Mars who has built up a pretty thorough collection of earth mammals.

The Martian zookeeper has noted some interesting things about the residents of the human exhibit. In the first place, compared to other creatures, their young are born alarmingly premature. Other mammalian newborns crawl to the mother's breast and begin to nurse, but if the human baby were not assisted to do this it would starve. The human baby takes a full year just to walk, an age at which—

even allowing for proportionate lifespans—other mammals are near adulthood. A human newborn looks like it's not ready to come out yet. But out it comes, and keeping it alive is an exhausting task for a very long time. It appears to be too much work for one parent.

The baby's ability to communicate in the language of the species is similarly slow to develop. Human parents are markedly more frustrated by inability to interpret their baby's cries than are bovine or canine mothers. Most mammals rapidly learn to survive without their mother's care, but a human may take decades of training before he is able to support himself.

The Martian notes that raising a human baby is a lengthy and exhausting process. Unlike the rearing of other mammals, it requires the attention of an adult nearly full-time; without that attention, the species would not survive.

It seems that the female is more suited to this intensive labor of childrearing, both by temperament and by her ability to nurse—an attribute so vital that it gives the mammalian family its name. Childrearing is so demanding that she has little time to provide food and shelter for herself, and both mother and child are at risk. The mother's arms encircle the child, but a second adult is required to add an outer ring of care around those two.

The child's father seems suited to this role, although not without ambivalence. The early years post-puberty, in particular, propel human males into an exhausting round of compulsive sexual thinking and (attempted) activity that was described by a satyriacal Hollywood star as "waking up every morning chained to a maniac." A look at these same males a few years later reveals that most have settled down in monogamous, childrearing arrangements, although some struggle against a recurrent longing for sexual adventure. What would motivate the males to accept such a trying bargain?

The zookeeper is not surprised that males wind up monogamous. The hand that designed the varieties of life in his zoo consistently shows exacting care for efficiency and symmetry. It would not have rigged a situation as counterproductive as a female who needs monogamous loyalty to produce the next generation and a male who flees it. Males must inevitably have a need for monogamy as well, although their motivation is not obvious.

The Martian zookeeper has developed some theories about why human males make this bargain. First, at the root, what feels like a sex urge is actually a reproductive urge. It will do the male no good to impregnate many women if these women are barely able to raise healthy children unaided. The children must survive and be strong enough to carry his genes forward one more generation for reproduction to have truly taken place.

Secondly, how can he know that the child his mate is raising does in fact carry his own genes, and not some other male's? Ultimately, he can only trust her word on this. In order to persuade her to mate only with him, he must offer her inducements: shelter, provisions, protection, and, perhaps most difficult, his own fidelity in pledge. As he watches the mother nurse their child, he sees his only link to the chain of human life. Without his connection to the two of them, he would free-fall into oblivion.

Is biology destiny? No; we are not prisoners of these roles, and our ingenuity can offer many ways to redesign them. But biology is orderly. It has its own internal logic, and when we tamper with one element of it we must expect another element to fall out of place. The superwoman single-mom with a hot career and a hot date is famously exhausted on her treadmill. This should not be surprising. Disrupt biology's rules and you will find yourself doing things a less-efficient way.

THE OTHER THING THE MARTIAN zookeeper notes is the heightened sense of loneliness humans display. They carry a burden of self-awareness that other mammals appear to evade, with associated fears of abandonment, rejection, and meaninglessness. They need more complex things from each other than goats do. Even in old age he sees them in pairs, when the impetus of childrearing is decades past. Gliding over earth's atmosphere in his shiny saucer, he observes elderly couples on Florida sidewalks wearing identical clothing. What's that all about?

The Martian is recognizing the profound human need for connectedness, and pregnancy is the icon of human intimacy. The connection an unborn child experiences with her mother is the first any human has of closeness to another person. Because it predates language and self-awareness, it is the more profound and ineradicable, though we may be largely unaware of this pull.

Life outside the womb is lonely. We look all our lives for an experience of similar intimacy and safety, even though many, as the saying goes, look in all the wrong places. When pregnancy begins, a woman is plunged into an experience of intimacy more profound than any of her adult life; she is knit, literally, to another human, one half-made of her own self. In the same blow she is linked to the child's father, whose half-life lives on as well within her body. Yet this being formed of two halves is more than their sum, a radical third never before seen on earth. She shoots from her parents' bodies like an arrow from a bow, carrying their immortality into the future, beyond the reach of their crumbling arms.

Pregnancy is about connectedness. It spins the wheel tighter, and centrifugal force draws the players together, more aware than ever of their mutual dependence. When a pair-bond is healthy, pregnancy makes it stronger still. Pregnancy problems have to do with broken connections: broken trust, fear, loneliness, abandonment.

When trust is risky, suspicion looks like wisdom. Abortion-rights rhetoric recognizes this and urges the woman to think only of her-self—my body, my rights, my decision. Those first-person-singulars tell a story. This viewpoint twists necessity into a virtue, and offers a wry consolation prize: life as a steely atom, spinning without con-tact, without the dangerous and tender cloak of skin. If pregnancy turns a wheel that draws all together, abortion breaks the wheel, spinning the participants out into isolation. It severs the woman at one blow from the child who trusts her, and from the man she wants to trust.

Yet even these guarded and isolated beings keep returning to each other for sex. That urge is hard to suppress, even when trust is absent and reproduction is vehemently unwanted. So why don't they use each other for passing sex, and prevent pregnancy with contraception? Wouldn't that make everybody happy?

The Martian zookeeper is perplexed to observe that this seem-ingly logical idea doesn't work in practice. Even though these hu-mans "don't want" to have unplanned pregnancies, even though contraception is cheap, available, and more effective than nothing, humans often choose not to use it. It looks to him as if sex is an-other one of those things that is more complicated for humans than it is for other creatures.

Unreckoned with in the contraceptive strategy—indeed, nearly unrecognized in thirty years of sexual revolution—is the distinctive character of women's sexuality. As feminist poet Adrienne Rich writes, "The so-called sexual revolution of the sixties [was] briefly believed to be congruent with the liberation of women. . . . It did not mean that we were free to discover our own sexuality, but rather that we were expected to behave according to male notions of sexuality."

What might be elements of authentic female sexuality? Germaine Greer wrote, "Women's desire for affection and closeness usually has to be translated, more or less unconsciously, into desire for sex." As the old cliché has it, girls give sex in order to get love; boys give love in order to get sex. When the sexual revolution flooded the market with "free sex," its trading equivalency in square units of love was radically depreciated.

Women are getting less and less durable love in return for sex, and some are suspecting they made a bad bargain. A poignant indicator is the finding that 84% of sexually active young teen girls, when asked what topic they wanted information about, checked, "How to say no without hurting the other person's feelings." It used to be that "nice girls don't"; now, being nice means you have to. Likewise, 83% of sexually experienced upperclassmen at inner-city high schools said that the best age to begin having sex was older than they had been.

Little girls have been catapulted into experiences they can't handle and don't enjoy (young teen boys not being known for their sensitivity or expertise) by the adult insistence that they're going to do it anyway. This insistence, one teen girl tells me, rings like a command: you *will* have sex—it's the law.

For adult women, the benefits of "free sex" have not been better than they were for teens. The consumer culture, which has found sex to be the magic bullet that sells anything, continues to promote compulsive, nearly compulsory sexual activity as the norm. As sexuality is snipped from the fabric of personhood and isolated as sheer mechanical act, severed from context and emotional ties, women are lonelier than ever. The self-help shelf in any bookstore is crowded with titles explaining How to Keep Your Man, How to Get Over Your Man, and How to Learn to Trust Men Again. Apparently this is a boom market.

WHILE THE LIBERAL SIDE of this dialogue promotes con-traception, conservatives have a different plan for preventing un-planned pregnancies, but it doesn't center on contraception. Instead, it is concerned with responding more accurately to women's trust-based sexuality. Taking into account her need for emotional secu-rity, plus the indications that childrearing requires two parents, strategists have cooked up a notion to cover all bases. They call it "marriage."

The very term is enough to provoke sneers among the elite. Marriage can't be the answer; it disappoints, is imperfect, demands annoying sacrifices, limits one's range of sexual adventure. The pre-ferred way of stating this is "Ozzie-and-Harriet is a myth," an oddly naive protest. Those who are startled to find that marriage isn't like a chuckling fifties sitcom are going to be disappointed to real-ize that clapping their hands doesn't bring Tinkerbell back to life, either.

But it is currently fashionable to see the nuclear family as the repository of evil. Thus we hear that "96% of families are dysfunc-tional," an item of statistical absurdity comparable to "96% of people are too short."

In fact, the nuclear family is not a wacky new untested idea, prone to damage participants virtually every time. There are many centuries of evidence showing how the concept works in practice: pretty well, usually resulting in the survival and success of a new generation, humankind's first responsibility. Bonuses of compan-ionship, romantic love, pleasure, and joy often appear as well.

In comparison, an ethic of sexual freedom, where one in four pregnancies ends in abortion and the number of children in single-parent homes keeps rising, fails this goal like clockwork. Indicators for sexually transmitted disease, divorce, abandonment, impover-ishment of women and children, unwed motherhood, and abortion are at record levels; the heartbreak index is at an all-time high. Despite all this pursuing of happiness, Americans appear to be, by every reasonable standard, markedly more unhappy. The flip side of freedom is loneliness.

Those who sold the sexual revolution as a blessing for women turned out to be no friend of womankind; those who opposed it turned out to be no enemy. There may be a reason why the feminist movement arose on the cultural left, not the right: men on the left are harder on women. Left-wing men expect women "to behave according to male notions of sexuality," while men on the right more generally uphold woman-friendly notions of chastity, fidelity, lifelong marriage, and so forth. Every few years a study comes out showing, to general amazement, that devoutly religious married women report the highest levels of sexual satisfaction. Maybe it shouldn't be so hard to figure out.

The sexual revolution made the promise that we were entitled to fun without consequences, but that was nonsense along the lines of "You can eat banana splits all day without gaining weight." In real life, actions have consequences, and they can't be warded off by crying, "Hey, no fair!" If it hurts enough, we can stop now.

But these are not matters for public policy. We cannot pass laws to induce people to behave responsibly and honor their commitments. Such self-sacrificial changes come only when people have determined that the course that promised pleasure is instead bringing pain. Changing behavior comes from changing minds, which can be a sometimes easy, sometimes impossible task.

A FEW YEARS AGO the moderate-left Progressive Policy Institute sponsored a forum titled "Fortifying the Family," which presented the daring idea that children are better off with two parents. T. Berry Brazelton, Barbara Whitehead, William Galston, and others argued eloquently that children need intact families.

I sat near a woman who carried a journalist's notepad and who was not having fun. She passed the morning scowling at the floor, tapping her pencil, tapping her foot, and emitting derisive snorts. When others applauded, she hugged her legal pad to her chest. I guessed that she had made some choices in her life that did not follow the proposed direction, and as a result was not feeling adequately affirmed.

When the question period began, she raised her hand. She confessed herself "nervous" at the promotion of two-parent families, and informed the crowd that "Ozzie-and-Harriet is a myth."

I presume that when she left the conference she wrote a news story about it. How do you think it read? What assumptions did readers absorb?

People often plead for stable marriages on the basis that they benefit children, but children are not the ones we need to convince. Kids already know that they want both a mommy and a daddy. The harder task is convincing grownups who have made different choices and now feel compelled to defend them, who, when they hear the two-parent model celebrated, feel scourged as failures. How can we expect the elite of the media, education, and government to promote values they are unready to meet in their personal lives?

It is hard to gain public approval of any moral conviction in such circumstances. For example, the idea that teens should be taught to abstain from sex before marriage is attacked, not by teens, but by adults; they protest that expecting abstinence is unrealistic. They may be trying on the advice personally, and concluding it would be unrealistic for themselves. They may also be feeling something like the sting of personal insult. A public-school teacher who taught her middle-schoolers the reasons to abstain from sex outside marriage received angry calls from parents: "Don't teach my kids to judge how I live!"

Arguments in favor of marriage are often couched in terms of the effect on children. The threat is: Stay together or you'll damage your kids. But there is a promise as well: the inherent joy and goodness possible in marriage, the love that makes the couple the beating heart of a two-parent home.

The image of marriage has been so distorted that it will take some work to recover. Currently there are only two varieties of couple-family our culture can imagine: shiny-glib TV-show heaven, or grim, abusive horror-show hell. Real marriage, marriage that lasts, is neither.

If Tolstoy is right that "happy families are all alike," perhaps they are alike in not expecting to be happy all the time. Perhaps they expect to meet problems and disappointments and take them in stride. In real marriage—not the TV-show or horror-show versions—the dishes get dirty, the wife gets plump, the husband gets bald, and everyone gets grumpy at least occasionally. In the course of a lifetime together, everyone will need forgiveness, and happy families learn that giving it is the best way to ensure receiving it in return.

Why put up with these annoyances? For one thing, it is far worse to be alone. The world is too big and we are too small to make it through without being trampled. The bravado of individualism is false; we can never be free enough to be all-powerful, but we can be free enough to be lost. We warm our hands together at the night fire. Behind the other's back we see, behind our own back we know, the dark wilderness broods.

"It is not good for man to be alone," but it is also positively good to be together. The light you loved in your lover's eyes at the beginning grows more compellingly beautiful through the years. You meet those eyes in worship, in passion, in anger, in tears, over the baby's bassinet, over your father's casket. There is no substitute for the years, the lifetime work, of looking into those eyes. Gradually, you see yourself there; gradually, you become one.

Consumer culture relentlessly tells us that what we want is to wake up next to someone sexy tomorrow morning. In the quiet of our hearts we know: We want to wake up next to someone kind, fifty years from tomorrow morning.

When sexual activity is kept within the bounds of lifelong commitment, babies are more likely to survive and women more likely to feel secure and loved. The person unconsidered so far in this scenario is the man, the father of the child. What's in it for him? Don't men's desires run to sexual adventuring, spurning hearth and home?

IN A TONY SEAFOOD RESTAURANT in the suburbs of Washington, DC, our dinner business meeting is running late. As we hammer out the course of a proposed magazine article, three male leaders of the pro-family movement are trying to convince me of the persistence of male sexual incorrigibility. Men are shallow, self-centered, and interested only in the next exploit, they tell me. They will inevitably use women and dump them without a backward glance. "Men just want to do it and run," one states bluntly.

I look at three tired faces, winding up another long workday. In three suburban homes, these men's wives are tucking in the cumulative nine children and ending busy workdays of their own—days they could spend at home because their husbands are still wearing ties at 9:00 PM.

I think about sheep in wolves' clothing. I ask my dinner

companions why, if they are such barely restrained fiends, they are going home tonight instead of running off with a perky office intern. They register surprise. Because the risks are too high and the benefits too low. Because they delight in their homes and children. Because they feel pride in protecting and providing. Most of all, because they love their wives.

THE MARTIAN PONDERS the white-haired man on the sidewalk. He is baking in the Florida sun, waiting outside the craft shop while his wife gathers materials to make another ceramic doll. His lime-green polo shirt and white slacks match her own.

His children are grown, his youth is gone, twenty thousand days and nights of marriage have flown past. His days of power, of protecting and providing, have slipped away. He waits quietly in the sun, a little drowsy. There is no reason on earth for him to be there but one.

14 | FRATERNIZING WITH THE ENEMY

I ARRIVED A LITTLE EARLY to pick up my eleven-year-old son at church camp. It was dinnertime in the long wooden hall, 263 kids noisily banging the cups and wolfing down cherry cobbler. Suddenly a table of boys burst into incoherent song—the words a blur, but the tone tauntingly playful. It was greeted with a mixture of applause and boos. "That's Cabin 44," Stephen grinned. "Every night they have a battle with Cabin 5. They make up rhymes about each other."

When a few minutes had elapsed another song struck up, this one all in girls' voices. "That's Cabin 5," Stephen told me. When they finished, I joined the yays (Go, team!) while Stephen went "Boo!" "I had to go 'Boo,'" he explained to me, sincerely. "I knew they were making fun of men. I knew it was a sexist joke."

Where did this come from? Playful sparring between boys and girls is sexist? What next?

The war between the sexes is probably the first conflict we encounter in life. I recalled the day my daughter had come home from first grade, her face red with fury. A boy had said something very bad to her; she was so angry she couldn't bear to repeat it. With my coaxing, it eventually came forth. What the boy had said was,

"Girls go to Jupiter to get more stupider.
Boys go to Mars to get more candy bars."

Now, this does not impress me as an example of high-flown devastating rhetoric, but it had its desired effect on my daughter. The war was on.

It is a given that, in this vast and lonely world, people enjoy finding a place by identifying with a group, and exaggerating differences with those outside the group. But why is the first such group-division we encounter that of girls versus boys? As I looked across that dining hall, I saw lots of ways the children could have divided up against each other. As it was an Orthodox church camp, I could see children with Lebanese, Greek, and Slavic features, in addition to Oriental- and African-Americans and blue-eyed Anglo-Saxons like my son. It would have been easy to choose sides according to ancient ethnic feuding lines. Alternatively, we were just a stone's throw from the Mason-Dixon line; all these now-American children could have squared off as Northerners versus Southerners. Or the older adolescents could have tormented and abused the younger kids. Any number of conflicts could have been chosen.

But it was Cabin 44 versus Cabin 5, and I think this is because the difference between boys and girls is one that is ultimately good news. That boys and girls are different is a fact for rejoicing, a truth that leads quite literally to life, lots more of it, for generations to come. Girls versus boys is the division-by-groups that is most fun to play at.

This is what gender differences are all about. Sex differences are a matter of bare biology, something physically indisputable. Gender differences are embroidery; they are what a culture invents to celebrate those basic "vive la difference"s.

For the most part, gender differences are a good thing, delightful, playful, and enjoyable. When they take a darker form, when they are used to oppress, that evil should be named and challenged. But it's a mistake to begrudge gender differences entirely, and throw the baby out with the pink- or blue-trimmed bassinet. The first thing we want to know about a new baby is "boy or girl?" because it's fun that there are both kinds in the world, and it's fun that they are different from each other.

Sex differences are a very good thing, the means by which the human race goes on. Healthy cultures instinctively recognize and celebrate them. There's no point in being resentful of this playful impulse. A professor was telling me recently that a visiting expert had pointed out to her students the many "sexist" terms in our language. "All the nicknames for women, like 'chick' or 'kitten,' are diminutive," she said. "I *am* diminutive," I said. "I'm five-foot-one." Why pretend otherwise? How does it hurt me? And, as my grandmother told me, it's an advantage to be short because you can dance with all the boys. She knew what made the world go 'round.

Those who crusade against gender differences seem to mean, in practice, that women should reject femininity. There was a time when it meant also that men should reject masculinity, and I'm delighted that time has passed. The seventies-style man who was touchy-feely made me feel creepy-crawly. Now it's a one-way street; only one type of personal style is admired, and it is tough, lean, and has a firm, authoritative voice. Men do this with apparent ease. Women do it awkwardly and unconvincingly. Forced, tough women are to natural men as beef jerky is to beef. There is a kind of natural womanly strength, seen in Christians like Mother Teresa, St. Nina of Georgia, and St. Thekla—a mingling of boldness, integrity, and compassion which is equal to any man's. It just has no need to swagger and spit to prove its toughness; it is not concerned with being graded on any masculine scale.

Gender differences are rooted in an exaggeration of sex differences, and we enjoy those differences all our lives, long after we stop sending each other to Jupiter. After all, most of men's and women's bodies are *not* different. The bare truth is that we are as alike as Rome and Macintosh apples, and there is far more that is in common—eyes, hands, appendixes—than there is that is unique.

So it is those unique characteristics that get the most emphasis: women wear waist-cinching outfits that allude to the hourglass shape, no matter what shape the lady inside; men's suits boast brawny, padded shoulders. A woman's skin is really only slightly softer than a man's, but she will work diligently to heighten that difference, while declining to develop rocky biceps. We exaggerate the differences, while tacitly ignoring the 98% we hold in common. I don't see anyone trying to enlarge their ears.

All across the clamorous dining hall, kids were ignoring other divisions of color, age, region, or ethnicity. The marker each had chosen to highlight was the most benign, most joyful one of all—the good news of being boys and girls. Much has been written in recent decades about this eternal war between the sexes, and too much of it has been bitter and sour. Where women have been unjustly prevented from the opportunity to rise to the height their talent deserves, justice is not served, and such wrongs must be righted. But the deeper, mischievous war is too much fun to end. As the old saw goes, there will never be a victory in the war between the sexes; there's too much fraternizing with the enemy. We wouldn't have it any other way.

15 | WHO'S TAMING WHOM?

IT'S A MAN'S WORLD, at least around my house. With my daughter off at college, it's just my husband, two teenaged sons, and me; even the dog and cat are of the masculine persuasion. Now, I've seen some majority-male households that have slipped toward caveman conditions, where underwear is washed by wearing it in the shower and dishes are washed by giving them to the dog. I'm determined that that won't happen here.

Rather than draw up a long list of rules covering tiny aspects of behavior, I've found that one general principle covers all circumstances. It's one my boys actually came up with on their own. The rule is (and this must be hissed in an urgent whisper): "Not in front of the chick!"

Yes, in my house, as far as I know, no one drinks from the milk jug. No one burps. Dignity and decorum rule the day. When I phone home from a business trip, I can almost hear the dishes being whisked out of the living room and the orange juice being wiped off the kitchen floor. The dog, I am given to understand, has been creating these unauthorized situations, grievous and clearly unworthy of chick review. Good thing my boys are there to maintain order. "Bad Sparky!" I hear over the phone line, and picture the bewildered dog ducking his head.

The most obvious charge one could lay against this standard is that it's sexist, and indeed it is. The "Not in front of the chick" rule colludes in a tacit assumption that how men behave when they are alone together might be different from how they behave in feminine company. It presumes that men and women are different, men naturally devolving to a rougher state if given the chance. Women demand something finer of them: respect, protection, the kind of cherishing (St. Paul suggests) which men give to their own bodies.

This is a positive thing. When men *don't* feel an obligation to protect and cherish women, women get hurt. Men come to look out on a leveled world, and treat everyone the way they treat each other—that is, pretty rough. The interaction of guys in my house tends toward broad insults, punches, and grins. They thrive on it, but girls whose exchanges regularly ran to, "Well, your nose is bigger!" would not be friends long.

Recognizing the relative roughness of men blends well with the theory put forth by George Gilder in *Men and Marriage*, that men must be civilized by women. Men's natural impulse is to stray and play, he says, and it is due to women's influence that they settle down in families and contribute to a coherent society. Without this taming, men would wreak havoc.

Yet I've always thought there was an element of polite fiction to this formulation. Men seem to settle down into families willingly enough; at some level, it must be what they want to do. When they attribute their domestication to the fair sex's beguilements, it is flattering to both. The lady gets to be the fair angel of the hearth, whose purity and cleverness ensnared the savage beast. He gets to be a rough-hewn lusty fellow, whose caveman ways are barely held in check by the lady's silken cords. As he pushes the lawnmower on Saturday afternoon, the sun reddening his bald spot, he can think:

I might look like Harry Homeowner, but inside I'm still a wildman. If I didn't have to fix the dryer vent, I'd be zooming down the California coast on a Harley.

Not that there isn't plenty of historical evidence for men being the sex that is most likely to wreak havoc. Women do appear to be more genteel. When we read a newspaper account of a gory crime, we're never shocked to discover that the culprit is male. As author Joel Achenbach says, we're accustomed to "Male Pattern Badness."

Yet women need improving, too. Their badness-pattern is not as showy as men's, but it has its own distinctive malevolence. While boys are asserting rank by beating up the slight or wimpy kids, girls are wounding their unattractive or clumsy classmates with teasing, malicious gossip, and humiliating practical jokes. Boys, at least, are direct. Victims of girl-style viciousness know that words can do more lasting hurt than sticks and stones. The tenderness females are famed for may go no deeper than the skin.

The problem with the caveman-and-angel scenario is that it gives too much moral credit to women. Women aren't intrinsically superior to men, nor are they programmed with better virtues. When a man falls, it can't be blamed on a wife failing to train him. Likewise, a woman's flaws can't be blamed on men. But in marriage, each spouse has a responsibility to help the other grow in character, now exhorting, now encouraging, as needed.

It may well be that women have a special calling to tame men, to refine the brutish aspects of their nature by holding them to a gentler standard. Even a mild reminder like prohibiting certain habits "in front of the chick" is a step of progress.

But men have a calling to tame women as well. Woman's vaunted compassion is the sunny side of a tendency that, on its darker side, makes moral evaluations based on emotion or what "feels right inside." What feels right is notorious for collapsing into what merely feels good. It may feel good to torment another little girl in class, or to hide the last piece of pie to enjoy alone later, or to flirt with an ugly boss and edge out a coworker for promotion. Whatever pleases me feels good, and so I presume that it is good. Scarlett O'Hara could give us a lesson about this.

Men, for all their faults, are less likely to be confused by slippery emotion. Men's vilified judgmentalism is the darker side of a tendency that, on its positive side, makes moral evaluations based on objective right and wrong, that shows a hunger for fairness and balance. It is rightly suspicious of merely heart-driven ethics, because the heart is so stubbornly convinced that charity begins at home.

Men need us women to soften them up, gentle and tame them; we women need men to remind us of the rights of others, to make us play fair, and to tame us as well. It's clear that we need each other. You'd almost think someone planned it that way.

16 | MEN NEED CHURCH, TOO

NEXT TIME YOU'RE IN CHURCH, count the number of adult heads and divide by the number of pairs of pantyhose. If the pantyhose contingent makes up more than half the total, there's a word for your church: typical.

"Every sociologist, and indeed every observer, who has looked at the question has found that women are more religious than men," writes Leon Podles in his book, *The Church Impotent*. (Ouch; the stentorian title makes me wince. Once inside, however, it's reasonable and well-written.) Podles cites a deluge of statistics: In 1986 church growth expert Lyle Schaller observed 60% female to 40% male churchgoers, a split which has widened since. Jesuit theologian Patrick Arnold says he's found a female-to-male ratio ranging from 2:1 to 7:1, and "some liberal Presbyterian or Methodist congregations are practically bereft of men." Even in churches that have an all-male ordained leadership, the inner circle of laity that actually runs things is likely to be mostly female. Sociologist Edward H. Thompson states that "throughout all varieties of black religious activity, women represent from 75 to 90 percent of the participants." These are observations based on attendance, but the last time a census of membership by gender took place was 1936. Even back then women outnumbered men across denominations, with Pentecostals almost 2 to 1.

On the one hand, these figures are good news. The faith that raised the status of women in the ancient world still raises their spirits today, and it's hard for anti-Christian snipers to claim that Christianity is anti-women when women fill pews so enthusiastically. As John Updike wrote in a recent issue of *The New Yorker*: "It is not Christianity that condoned, as late as 1910, foot-binding, a fashionable torture inflicted on female children, or the habit of female infanticide, which skews China's gender balance even now. It is not Christianity that in parts of Africa promotes clitoridectomy as a means to properly shaped femininity. It is not Christianity that inflicts upon women, as in Iran and Afghanistan, hysterical restrictions that inhibit their access to employment, education, social life, and even medical care."

But why aren't men there in equal numbers? It's not accurate to say men aren't as interested in religion, since they participate strongly in Islam and Judaism. Podles suggests that Christian congregations outside Europe and America enjoy better balance, and cites the Polish Solidarity workers who boldly displayed their faith. But somewhere along the line, Western Christian faith lost some of its manly appeal.

The Norman Rockwell painting, "Easter Morning," depicts the problem: Dad slouches in his pajamas, awash in newspapers, while Mom and the kids march past him in their Sunday best. A hundred years before that, clergy were already being stigmatized as prissy and effeminate. In the late seventeenth century Cotton Mather complained that only women came to church. Following the evidence back through history, Podles arrives at the thirteenth century, when St. Bernard of Clairvaux developed a mysticism based on imagining oneself the Bride of Christ.

Where St. Paul had described a bridal role for the entire Church, the nuptial bond was now imagined as me-and-Jesus alone, and swoony with passion. Women, then enjoying a period of increased freedom, popularized this approach, but men found it harder to imagine themselves in Jesus' arms. Yet the notion took hold, persisting through the centuries: even stern Cotton Mather taught that Jesus marries each individual believer, and Promise Keepers' Bill McCartney said we should "be in a love affair with Jesus." The empty receptiveness of Mary supplanted the sacrificial obedience of Jesus as the model for all Christians, a passivity many men found emasculating. Perhaps in reaction they retreated into ever-dryer forms of scholasticism, and for the first time theology was divorced from devotion.

Men still feel the need for transcendent meaning, Podles says, but if the only faith they see is soft and sappy, they'll seek it elsewhere: through career power, competitive sports, or, when particularly belittled or hopeless, through violence, drugs, and danger. As they slipped out the back door of the church, more seats were occupied by women. In the fourteenth century the rate of saints canonized that were women rose from 50% to 71%, and remaining male saints were not laymen, but monks and clerics. Heart won and head lost, which is why centuries later your church has twenty-seven sopranos and three basses.

The statistics above suggest the gap is widening, perhaps accelerated by the context of consumerism. Advertising leads us to think of our desires as important and precious things, and to expect to be wooed. We assume that God's relationship with us is based on His desire to console and reassure us, rather than our desperate need to be rescued from sin and conformed to His holiness. But throughout the New Testament and for a millennium, the Gospel message of consolation was matched by "masculine" calls to strive like an athlete and to lay aside sin.

Perhaps the Church's message needs to be gender-adjusted. We can try changing the sign in front of the church from "We Care About You!" to "Faith Demands Things of You!" Then be prepared to include a choir budget item: You'll need more music stands for the basses.

17 | PERILS OF PIZZA DELIVERY

WHEN MY DAUGHTER GOT A JOB delivering pizzas, I was a little concerned. Is the neighborhood safe? Do they deliver after dark? I imagined her standing in a shadowy hallway all alone, vulnerable to any sort of mayhem, and armed only with a pizza.

She came home from the first day at work with reassuring news. "They don't take any chances," she said. "If they have any questions about the call, they won't send me. They'll send one of the guys."

I felt ambivalent. I was glad that my daughter would be reasonably safe. But now I was imagining some boy in a greasy pizza-delivery smock standing in that same shadowy hallway, with skin no more bulletproof than my daughter's. He would go in her place, if there was any chance of danger. I didn't even know his name.

We hear plenty of persistent, and sometimes justified, complaining that women get a raw deal in life, that men get all the breaks. But we forget one thing guys do for us, without thinking, over and over again. It's something we expect from them; we may even take it for granted. We expect them to risk their lives.

It's part of the guy job description. Whenever there's danger, any man is expected to protect any woman at any cost. This is true no matter who she is; it's not an honor awarded only to his wife or daughter. I remember reading about two reporters who were mugged on a city street; the man leapt in front of the woman to take a fatal bullet. It struck me as a noble gesture, but one which followed the natural order of things. It wasn't until I tried to imagine her leaping in front of him that I realized the size of the sacrifice. It's just what we expect men to do.

Does this mean that we value women's lives more than men's? We certainly seem more comfortable risking men's lives, whether in war or firefighting or pizza delivery. When you stop and think about it, it's a pretty impressive gift for one gender to give another.

I think about all the men who have reflexively protected me all my life, hard-wired by genes and training to do so. Guys darting ahead of me up the stairs of a parking garage, or getting imperceptibly larger as we walk down a dark street, as if they were being inflated with an air hose. Sometimes their worry seemed silly to me, and I accepted it with a sigh, as my children react to my worrying over them.

Men's urge to protect women must feel something like women's urge to protect our children. My urge to protect my daughter—and my son. I wonder what sorts of jobs he'll have when he's a little older. One thing's for sure. I don't want him delivering pizza.

18 | SAFE-T-MAN

IT'S NOT EVERY DAY you get to see a photo of a woman folding a man up and pushing him into a suitcase. But there she is: standing outside a compact car, shoving an amiable-looking fellow in a rugby shirt into a carrying case.

Make that a "#4858944 Zippered Nylon Carrying Tote." Yes, this is Safe-T-Man, the inflatable bodyguard, "a life-size, simulated male that appears to be 180 lbs. and 6 ft. tall."

It's apparent that this product, advertised in airline in-flight catalogs, is aimed at women. Women, that is, who live alone. With his "positionable latex head and hands" Safe-T-Man can ride along beside you in your car looking jaunty, as here, in mirrored sunglasses and a leather jacket. Or he can sit at your breakfast table at home, carefully posed near the window; here he wears a jacket and tie and brainy-guy glasses, and studies the *Daily News*.

Doesn't look like much companionship, but that's not the point. Safe-T-Man is designed "to give others the impression that you have the protection of a male guardian with you."

Now, wait a minute. Male guardian? Why does it have to be male? Why not female, or animal or vegetable, for that matter? I thought that, in the memorable feminist jibe, "A woman needs a man like a fish needs a bicycle." So why would a woman's guardian have to be an inflatable man?

Oh yeah—protection. That old thing. Men are still generally bigger and stronger than women, so a woman with a man next to her just feels safer than a woman alone. Sure, she could be accompanied by another woman, or a poodle, or a really large cauliflower, but it isn't the same. When it comes to protection, there's no good substitute for a man.

Maybe we do need them after all.

It seems like every time we modern women nearly wrestle Nature to the ground, shouting "Biology is not destiny!", it springs up again saying, "Oh, yes I am." It will take some powerful rhetoric to convince our genes that men are not bigger than we are. That having them on our side isn't actually in our interest.

Safe-T-Man brought again to mind the tendency over the last couple of decades for men to be belittled and criticized by our culture, while women are exalted—in the jargon of the movement, "valorized." We don't need men, the notion goes: women are perfect and men are creeps, men just complicate women's lives, and we're better off without them. Sitcoms and comic strips generally portray men as idiots, and women as long-suffering figures of wisdom.

Maybe it's me, but I just don't see it. In my part of the country there are lots of men—about half the population, I guess. In fact, men live in houses on both sides of me, and even in my own home. I've had lots of opportunities to observe them, and they look okay to me. I feel safer with them around, not burdened or annoyed. In fact I've found that, if you get a real-live man and not one of the vinyl variety, he can open jars, tote the new dryer into the basement, and change your flat tire on an icy day. Mine even cooks.

But even men have accepted the idea that their gender is

contemptible. I heard about Safe-T-Man from a friend: he says it indicates "the lack of solid, dependable men" in women's lives.

But he himself is a solid, dependable man, gracing the life of his wife and their kids. In my neighborhood, in my church, everywhere I see lots of these, including single men still searching for a bride. It's not that great men aren't out there, though linking up with the right one can be tricky. But it doesn't help when women deny their existence and, sour-grapes fashion, insist we don't need them.

There's no doubt that a market for Safe-T-Man indicates a failure for men and women to form successful long-term relationships. The state of courtship and marriage in the U.S. is indeed confused. But a good first step might be: Ladies, stop pretending we don't need guys. Give them the respect any human deserves, and they'll live up to it. Most of them are already living up to it, even in the face of habitual scorn.

I saw a discarded lapel button, trodden in the snow, outside a card shop the other day; it read, "Tell me again why I need a man." Across the way, the card shop window was full of Valentines.

I like to think there's a connection.

19 | THE ONEIDA EXPERIMENT

IN THE MIDDLE OF THE ROOM there was a wood-burning stove. The small iron door was open on this chilly day, and the red flames could be seen leaping within as if in time to music. For there was music, too, a marching song, and the little girls who circled the stove marched around it in time. The girls were not happy.

Each girl was holding in her arms her favorite doll. These were pretty dolls with painted faces, who usually wore fancy clothes reflecting current fashion. But today the clothes had been left in a pile, and the wax figurines were exposed, hard and bare. One by one, each girl marched up to the open door of the stove. One by one, each girl threw her doll into the "angry-looking flames."

The phrase is that of Harriet Worden, a woman who participated in the sacrifice that day and recalled the painful event long after. It was 1851, in the utopian community of Oneida, in upstate New York. What was being burned up that day was an unseemly trait that their teachers had observed developing in the little girls of the commune. The dolls had become too important to the children; these were frivolous toys, indicating an affection for worldly finery and vain display. Women of Oneida were expected to bob their hair rather than fuss it to flattering styles, and to wear efficient clothing rather than long, sweeping gowns. They were to work in the factories alongside the men, while men took their equal share of labor in the kitchen. Pretty dolls were a tantalizing, subversive distraction.

But there was another concern: little girls were becoming attached to specific dolls. A child might choose one as her favorite, rock it and croon to it, tuck it in at night. This was a dangerous tendency.

Oneida was founded on the principle of "Bible Communism." Founder John Humphrey Noyes insisted that, under his personally devised philosophy, there were to be no selfish attachments, no hoarding of love. The tender affection a little girl might feel for a special, beloved doll had to be burned away. So each girl marched up to the oven door with her "long-cherished favorite" in her arms, then stared as the flames consumed it. "We . . . saw them perish before our eyes."

What was being burned up that day was the tendency for any human to form an intense and private bond with another. Noyes could not permit this, because he had put sexual freedom at the head of his agenda; he was the inventor of the term, "free love." The Yale Divinity School student and sometime Congregationalist minister believed that "complex marriage" was God's will, as indicated by the scripture, "in the resurrection they neither marry nor are given in marriage, but are like angels in heaven" (Matt. 22:30). (This may not be how most of us imagine the angels pass the time, but the American nineteenth century was a fertile time for private interpretations of the Bible.)

"The abolition of sexual exclusiveness is involved in the love-relation required between all believers by the express injunction of Christ and the apostles," Noyes wrote. "The restoration of true relations between the sexes is a matter second in importance only to the reconciliation of man to God."

"Sexual freedom" is a term that could suggest a carefree heedlessness that did not obtain at Oneida. A man wishing to enjoy the company of a specific woman would submit his request to an appointed official who kept a ledger of such engagements. This official would then present the request to the woman who was the target of the man's intentions, and she might agree or refuse as she chose, though agreement was the general rule. According to the records, most women had two or three visitors per week, and a popular young woman might entertain as many as seven.

The purpose of the ledger, however, was not to restrain the free exchange of sexual favors. Nor was it to track the fathers of children born in the community. Such a task would have been nearly impossible in any case, but considering the era and the circumstances, astonishingly few children were born. Noyes understood that, for a scheme of sexual freedom to succeed and not be overwhelmed by progeny, non-procreative sex must be absolutely required. This was accomplished through Noyes' command that men utilize a primitive method for the prevention of pregnancy. It was effective: over a twenty-year period, only thirty-five children were born in the community of a hundred adults.

The purpose of the ledger was not to restrain sexual freedom, but to ensure it, by monitoring whether any couples were becoming overly attached to each other. There was always the terrible danger that a man and woman might fall in love and begin consorting with each other to the exclusion of others. Such incipient selfishness had to be stamped out.

Noyes phrased it this way: "The new commandment is that we love one another . . . not by pairs, as in the world, but en masse." When a man confessed that he had fallen in love with a woman in the community, Noyes responded sharply, "You do not love her, you love happiness."

A policy of free sex sounds like a dandy idea to a great number of people, something on the order of free ice cream. What's the harm in it? "To be ashamed of the sex organs is to be ashamed of God's workmanship," said Noyes. It feels good, so do it. Love is a good thing, and the more people you love the better. Free sex speaks to all the popular virtues: generosity, tolerance, pleasure, broadening of experience, deepening of empathy. The tree is good for food, a delight to the eyes, and to be desired to make one wise.

Those who are old enough will recall the onset of the contemporary sexual revolution, back in the late sixties. The movement was heralded by a titillating novel, *The Harrad Experiment*, which imagined a program of intentional sexual freedom being staged on a college campus. It wasn't just racy stuff (though it was that), it was also a seriously advanced philosophical position, an example of progress marching on. As at Oneida, the sexual revolution was seen as an attribute of utopia. It was promoted in every form of media and entertainment, from "Make Love, Not War" buttons to the musical *Hair*.

We can gain some historical perspective by comparing this free-love message with another message popular at the time. Though it's hard to believe now, there was once a time when mind-altering drugs were recommended; they were thought to be actually *beneficial*. Promoting this view is how Harvard prof Timothy Leary won his fame. A drug like LSD was represented as "mind-expanding," and who could oppose expanding your mind? There was no doubt that drugs could induce altered states of consciousness, and it was claimed that these altered states would produce great art and deep thoughts. The enlightening effects supposedly produced by drugs were contrasted contemptuously with the effects of alcohol. Booze made you stupid and sloppy. Drugs made you wise.

This theory swiftly went down in flames. Nearly everyone with any contact with this experiment saw uncontrollably hallucinating, terrified friends carted into mental hospitals. Everyone knew someone who had been seriously, perhaps permanently, burned by drugs. It turned out that these chemicals didn't produce great art after all, but incomprehensible garbage. The deep thought looked stupid the next day. Of course, despite all this disillusionment, drug use didn't cease entirely, and the problem remains to this day. But drug use did lose its trendy glow. It became impossible to continue the pretense that drugs held promise of enlightenment.

It's important to note something here. Mind-altering drugs did not lose their status because of a clever anti-drug campaign, or hard-hitting public service announcements, or improved anti-drug legislation. They lost their cachet because they were found to be damaging. Drugs turned out to be not as advertised. The heartening news here is that it is possible for cultures to change for the better, once given a dose of truth. Like a body, a culture has an innate impulse to health. Though this can be subverted in a million ways, it can be nurtured as well. That should give us hope.

As we all know, however, the sexual revolution message was more successful than the pro-drug movement. While a measure of shame has been restored to taking drugs, sex outside of marriage is still viewed as a harmless pastime. One reason this revolution was so successful is that the locus of shame was shifted; not the practitioners, but those who oppose free sex, were supposed to be feeling shame. This was especially true during the first blush of this movement, when free sex was presented as just one more aspect of the cheerful, daisy-sprinkled, bell-bottomed sixties. Only sour-faced moralists would disapprove of anything so innocent and pleasant. They must think sex is dirty, it was presumed; they must have unresolved sexual hang-ups. Thus the tables were turned; to oppose the sexual revolution was to stand revealed as a cramped and dirty-minded snoop. An advocate of the revolution, on the other hand, was a free and healthy child of nature. In a clever twist, those who indulged in behavior previously thought shameful turned the weapon against traditional morality, and accused them of shameful thoughts.

Why didn't the sexual revolution meet the same fate as the drug movement? It was swiftly clear that drugs were damaging lives pretty severely, sometimes beyond repair. Free sex, on the other hand, appeared to be like that bowl of free ice cream. It was a distinct and severable experience, with no impact on any other part of life—mere pleasure, with no repercussions.

Of course, this isn't true; free sex has innumerable repercussions, physical, emotional, and spiritual, and they can replicate indefinitely through many lives, and even through generations (just look at the cost of growing up without a daddy). But these effects are delayed. If your friend took some bad acid it was evident within hours, and the sight could be enough to scare you off the stuff for good. But at the moment sex feels good, and it might feel good in memory for a while afterwards. Sometimes there are no perceived ill effects at all.

As Josh McDowell wisely asks teens, if you're doing it because it feels good, how long does it have to feel good? Fifteen minutes? The rest of the day? Does it have to feel good when you find out you have herpes? What about AIDS? When your lover tires of you and spreads gossip about your body, or your adequacy in bed? What about when you find out you started a baby? Or when your parents find out? When you walk into the abortion clinic? When you're a school dropout, raising a child as a single parent? How good does it have to feel now, to make up for how bad it'll feel then?

Similar questions apply to adults as well. Will it feel good to be alone at the end of your life because you always played around and never made a commitment? When you're middle-aged and saggy and can't attract lovers any more? Will it feel good when all the classmates at your thirtieth high school reunion are showing pictures of their grandchildren, and you're showing a picture of your dog? Will it feel good when you divorce? When you get to see the kids only on weekends? What about when your lover skips off to enjoy "free sex" with someone else, and you are left behind, a loser nobody loves? Those are the rules of the game, and anyone who plays can lose everything.

Reality has a way of freeing us from confusion. This happened quickly with drugs, but it's taking longer with sex. Yet there has already been a marked toning-down of the initial pro-free-sex rhetoric. For example, in the mid-seventies there was a bestseller titled *Open Marriage*, written by a couple who claimed that adultery strengthened their relationship. They made it sound so reasonable: husband and wife explained that extracurricular activities deepened their enjoyment of each other and enhanced their ties. No one could deny it was so, since they made the claim based on private experience. The book caused quite a stir, which faded a few years later when the couple divorced. The complex knots in the human heart—jealousy, insecurity, the craving to be loved exclusively—can't be untied by an act of will, no matter how lofty the sentiment.

This was why John Humphrey Noyes set a goal of combating possessive love, and why the little girls had to burn their dolls. It may look as if free sex is as innocuous as free ice cream, but it has reverberations that run all down human relationships, requiring distancing and independence where interdependence would be the natural norm. It requires shifts in the underlying ways we view each other and interact, and touches a wider range of human experience than would be initially thought necessary. The repercussions of free sex are not as immediately visible as those of mind-bending drugs; but, because they take longer to emerge, they resound more deeply.

The initial problem free sex poses is that the sexual urge is, at root, a reproductive urge. It is planted in us to ensure that we have children, that the human race goes on. The urge is strong because it is a survival urge, as strong as the impulse to eat, drink, and find shelter. This is not to say that everyone who is moved to have sex does so because he or she consciously wants to have a child. The contrary may well be true. Likewise, some may gobble a bowl of ice cream while hoping it has no effect on the waistline. Wishes to the contrary, our craving for yummy fats is strong because it is a command of basic nutrition; fats are necessary to our bodies' health, the basic energy fuel. We want it because of something our body commands from the depths, though our mind may have a very different intention.

Sex is most deeply about reproduction, and human reproduction is a long-term project. It requires ongoing attention from two adults, not just one. The human child is born vastly more unformed and immature than any other mammal, unable to communicate, unable to feed itself. It requires care so intensive that a single mother and child operating alone are a fragile family; they are vulnerable to too many kinds of danger, in the jungle, the Arctic, or the inner city. The mother needs a male to protect and provide for herself and the child; he needs to protect them, or the child will not survive and his deeper goal of reproduction will fail. The circle of man, woman, child is the basic unit of any human society.

Sex is about reproduction, and reproduction requires sex. Contrary to popular opinion, God is in favor of this. It was His idea, after all. He devised many different ways for creatures and plants to reproduce on this earth, and lots of them don't look like much fun. Probably there were more efficient ways—and certainly more dignified ways—that God could have designed for human repro-duction. But this funny business was His idea, and every indication is He meant us to enjoy it.

We're sometimes told that the historic Christian Church is op-posed to sex, but this is simply not true. Christians have always favored sex within marriage, but opposed its appearance in other situations, much as we approve water in a pitcher but oppose it in a basement. Sex within marriage is not merely permitted, but honored.

The icon known as "The Conception of the Theotokos" dem-onstrates this. "Theotokos" is the name Eastern Orthodox Chris-tians apply to the Virgin Mary; it means "God-bearer." An ancient heresy suggested that Mary bore only Jesus' humanity; the Church responded that no, she was the mother of the Incarnate God Himself.

The conceptions of St. John the Baptist and of Jesus are de-scribed in Scripture, and these rapidly became annual celebrations in the early Church. Not much later, the conception of Mary was honored as well. But although the Bible records a miraculous story surrounding the conception of Jesus, Mary was conceived in the regular way (albeit by aged, previously barren parents). The icon of the feast, accordingly, shows a married couple in the privacy of their bedroom. In my copy, Mary's parents, Joachim and Anna, are stand-ing on a blue carpet before their bed, which has a blue striped cover and an embroidered pillow. They look serious, yet tender. They are in a graceful embrace; Anna has stretched up on tiptoe to press her face against her husband's, with her arm around his neck. This is how the life of a daughter begins.

This is a popular icon in Orthodoxy, one often given as a wed-ding gift and hung near the marital bed. It is a reminder of the goodness of sexual love, and God's intention that we use it in joy.

But Christians do oppose the misuse of sex, including temporary heterosexual encounters that lack a wedding ring. This is an impulse associated more with men than with women. Some theorize that the male is programmed to impregnate as many women as he can, and the woman's task is to capture and domesticate him against his will. There's a flaw in this logic, however. Reproduction only succeeds if the child survives and grows up to reproduce again; this is much more likely to happen if the child has two parents. Nature is biased in favor of reproduction, and what serves it best we find deepest in our hearts.

Thus we find a profound, instinctive conspiracy that binds mother, father, and child ever closer together. When another item is moved to the top of the agenda—sex without commitment, sex without consequences—it flings them apart. A culture such as ours, which has been dominated by the notion of free sex for decades, makes at least three shifts to accommodate the demands of that ethic and to avoid the demands of the nuclear family. First, it must eliminate the requirement that some lasting, exclusive commitment (like marriage) be made before sex. Second, it must find a way to prevent or eliminate children conceived in these uncommitted sexual relationships. Third, it must train women to support themselves with no help from men.

As John Humphrey Noyes understood, one of the first things required is a valiant commitment to eradicating "selfish" love. For free sex to succeed, women and men must be willing to forgo deep emotional commitment to each other. Not that these connections never happen, but that they cannot be required as a prerequisite to sex. It is apparent that, under this arrangement, women lose. The old saying goes: Girls give sex in order to get love, boys give love in order to get sex. When the board at the commodities exchange reads "Free Sex," girls aren't getting a very good deal. A teenage girl told me that a friend had confided in her, "I slept with Rick last night. Do you think he likes me?"

Ironically, this kind of sexual availability was promoted by feminists a few decades ago as an aspect of women's equality and freedom. The double standard was decried, as well it might be, but the remedy suggested was that women adopt male values. If men want sex without commitment, it must be what women want too. The Playboy philosophy—sex without commitment—was transformed from an example of oppression to one of liberation.

Looking back on this from the vantage point of thirty years, I think we got conned. Women fell for a shell game, and gullibly assumed that male sexual values were better than their own traditional, self-protecting ones. And like many victims of a clever con game, they continue to tell themselves that they got a good bargain.

Some, even in the feminist camp, are rethinking this. How did that which purported to liberate women somehow end with women feeling more endangered than ever? Instead of women's bodies becoming more securely their own private possession, these bodies were presumed to be open for business, available for public evaluation and use. Sociologists like Deborah Tannen and Carol Gilligan began writing about women's tendency to frame all interactions in the context of human relationships, unlike men who were more able to run mental, emotional, and physical functions on separate tracks. Much more than men, women are apt to be thrown off balance when sex is snipped out of the fabric of personhood and isolated as sheer mechanical act. A sexuality that more accurately respects women's nature is going to look a lot more like the kind of commitment-based arrangement that our mothers, grandmothers, and their ancestors demanded. In the history of women's sexuality, free sex is a brief, crazy experiment, and it has failed.

Second, in order to implement a regime of free sex, the sex that takes place must be free of children. John Humphrey Noyes insisted that men practice "male continence," but many less onerous methods are available today. The pill, which made its debut in the early sixties, is widely credited with enabling the sexual revolution. It and other chemical and mechanical methods have enjoyed seasons of popularity, but nearly all come with side effects that can give pause. This should not be surprising. Fertility is a condition deeply inscribed in the female body, and chemicals and devices strong enough to overcome it are likely to have other effects as well. As a friend of mine said regarding the birth control pill, "Why would I put in my mouth something I wouldn't put in my compost heap?"

The method that has won widest approval is condoms, perhaps because they are cheap and require no prescription, and alone among all methods provide some protection against disease. They are not perfect, of course, and can fail in many ways; failure is most guaranteed when they are left in the drawer of the bedside table. For this is the feminists' greatest complaint against condoms: men don't want to use them. Since it is the one modern method that men control, their refusal leaves women unprotected. And refuse they do. Although condoms are available in small towns across the nation for less than the price of a pack of cigarettes, and their use is promoted as nearly a patriotic act, half of all women having abortions said they were using no prevention method at all during the month they got pregnant.

Even when contraception is used, it isn't always effective, as indicated by the other half of abortion customers. As Maggie Gallagher points out, if contraceptives properly used are 95% effective over a year, a sexually active woman who uses them faithfully over a 10-year period stands a 43% chance of getting pregnant at least once. Her chances jump dramatically if she uses them with less than exacting care.

But free sex requires freedom from babies, so the second, grimmer enabler of the sexual revolution is abortion. A million and a half of these are done every year, one for every four births. About three-quarters are performed on unmarried women, often signaling the sad end of a fleeting affair. There was a time, of course, when unexpected pregnancy would be the occasion of some fast maturing: a young man would do the right thing, marry and support his family, or a young woman would quietly have the baby out of town and place it for adoption. The availability of contraception has subtly changed the equation, though; it promises that people have the right to have sex without pregnancy. If contraception fails, the appearance of a pregnancy is felt as an injustice, and the baby viewed as a trespasser. In this perspective, abortion is a right.

One might charge that, though there are some parallels between Oneida's regime of free sex and that of the present day, no one would command children to burn dolls. The maternal instinct to bond with a child is not feared, but admired. We love children; we dote on them. Yet it seems to me that sometimes there is something unhealthy in the way we love them—perfect, beautiful children, wanted children, chosen children, the ones who survived when their unwanted siblings went in the abortion clinic dumpster.

We love children, all right, but not in their own right, with their own needs. We love them in the manner of Shel Silverstein's rhyme: "Do I like children? Yes I do! Boiled, baked, or in a stew!" We love children as consumer items: pets, toys, providers of entertainment and prestige to their owners. Their existence is permitted if they fit adults' plans—if adults want them. If they fail to please, the results are not pretty.

The change in the rate of child abuse over twenty years of abortion tells the story. In 1974, 60,000 cases were reported: over a thousand children were being battered each week. But hope was on the horizon: *Roe v. Wade* was only one year old. As availability of abortion spread, women could weed out the children they didn't want before birth. Soon, only wanted children would get born. A world of wanted children, as the slogan goes, would make a world of difference.

Two decades later, the world is very different. Every person in America under the age of thirty could have been aborted; every child, teen, and twenty-something living escaped that fate by being sufficiently "wanted." And the reported cases of child abuse inflicted on all these chosen children? After twenty years of abortion, it was still 60,000—except that was the figure for a single *week*. In 1994, the total number of reported child abuse cases was 3.1 million.

How can this be? Perhaps it's due to better reporting; perhaps people are under more stress. Perhaps the disintegration of the family means that parents pushed to the limit no longer have an aunt or grandma—or husband—to take the baby for a while. (Though single-mom households make up only 17% of the population, they account for 40% of reported child abuse.)

But a simple, seismic shift was contained in the very notion that children had to be "wanted" before they earned the right to live. Parents' pleasure superseded their offspring's right to breathe, and there was no reason this right would cease after birth. In fact, numerous studies confirm that the most "wanted" children are the most likely to be abused. As measured by parental eagerness for the child during pregnancy, the child's being named after a parent, the mother going early into maternity clothes, the percentage of "wantedness" among abused children is between 91% and 96%. Perhaps the higher the (unrealistic) expectation, the deeper the disappointment. A cuddly bundle of joy in the delivery room may not be so wanted at the age of Terrible Two, or five, or fifteen, and the parent's right to reject feels just as valid then as during the

Supreme-Court-sanctioned initial nine months.

Does our current free-sex utopia eradicate the maternal impulse by requiring little girls to throw their dolls into the fire? No, it does it by requiring grown women to throw their children away in abortion clinics; and if children are something to throw away before birth, they are never safe after.

Thirdly, if an ethic of free sex replaces the nuclear family, women must be able to support themselves with no expectation of help from a male partner. Popular imagination might suppose that a free-sex utopia like Oneida was a disorderly paradise of leisure, but such was not the case. Men and women trooped off to work together daily, and the many products of the Oneida community made it a highly successful economic concern. It remains so to this day, though company philosophy about employee behavior has become more conventional. (The Oneida silverplate platter remains a staple wedding gift, and every newborn needs an Oneida baby cup.) Oneidans were taught to expect women to labor at the same jobs as men, and men were required to share women's work in the communal kitchen.

A similar thing happened, of course, with the advent of the sexual revolution a few decades ago. The opportunities for women to compete in the public sphere have been a blessing, and I have been the beneficiary of groundbreaking work done by those women who demanded just such a chance. A problem can arise when the demand is not for a chance to compete, but for guaranteed success. I think this insistence on equality of outcome is a backhanded insult, implying that on a level playing field women couldn't compete. Speaking personally, being a woman has been far from a handicap, and is more like an advantage. Conservative, pro-life, and Christian groups, in my experience, go out of their way to give women a chance. Maybe on the other side of the fence sexism and anti-female bias are more common; women on that side are clearly

more touchy about it and more insistent on regulatory enforce-
ment of "fairness," suggesting that discrimination is a familiar problem.

A strong work ethic is, of course, not a bad thing. Where the
problem arises is when women are expected to provide for themselves without support from men, and where the thrill of a paycheck is supposed to be a substitute for long-term romance.

When free sex becomes the dominating social value, a society
must adjust in many ways. We've examined just three of them: dis-
couragement of a requirement of commitment before sex, methods
to avoid childbearing, and expecting that women be self-supporting.
All three of these were values championed by the feminist movement as essential to improving women's lives. Thirty years later, many
elements of women's lives—and those of men and children as well—
are worse. There has been an explosion of sexually transmitted
disease, single mothers and children living in poverty, child abuse,
teenage childbearing, divorce. It's not clear that anyone is happier.
Free ice cream has a high price.

The root problem is that it's not sex that animates us so, but
something deeper and more broad: *eros*. Sex and eros are not the
same thing. Sex is a physical act, but eros is the underlying emotional attachment, and it is much more powerful. Eros is the force
that makes you want to claim this man, or this woman, as your
own, and cling to him or her forever. It's exclusive, craving fidelity
and rejecting competitors.

John Humphrey Noyes knew it to be the ultimate enemy of
Oneida's dream, capable of wrecking his utopia of "free love." Sex
was to be spread abroad in that garden of delights, but true love was
the enemy. Eros commands with a more powerful voice than mere
physical appetite. And eros wins in the end.

Thirty years after they burned the dolls at Oneida, John

Humphrey Noyes' dream was falling apart. As an old man he had fled the grounds of the commune under cover of darkness, a step ahead of rumors that Oneida defectors were telling federal investigators that he had been having sex with underage girls. These charges were true. Though Noyes wrote exhortatory letters to his followers from exile, and many tried to follow his dream, the old longings for fidelity and marriage began appearing once more.

Before long, virgins were refusing to follow the custom of being initiated into sex by the older men; they were holding out for marriage. Women who had borne children out of wedlock now began refusing further sexual relations, likewise demanding a wedding ring and exclusive fidelity. Teenaged couples were falling in love and pledging fidelity to each other, against all the rules. Younger women began growing their hair out and wearing long-skirted dresses. Mothers would no longer allow communal child-care workers ultimate control over their children's lives, but demanded the right to raise them as they saw fit. The dream of "Bible Communism" was ending.

Women want to raise their own kids; it's a longing that can't be burned away as easily as burning a wax doll. Men love women, and feel a yearning they can hardly understand to select one and cherish her, provide for her, even risk their lives for her. We have tried for decades to burn away those longings by setting out bowls of free ice cream, and they have looked beguiling indeed, on movie screens, magazines, and MTV. But the body has an impulse to health, and can't live on ice cream alone. Pretty soon people start looking around for healthier fare. In the process they are apt to find each other, settle down, and form families once again. And in the heart of many a healthy family is a little girl holding a doll.

20 | OVERTHROWN BY EROS

AWHILE BACK, *THE NEW YORKER* magazine provided a 22-page look inside a strange world: the land of porn film production. Author Susan Faludi gave readers a sympathetic glimpse at the tough lot of a male porn star.

No, really. In this business, the woman is the object of desire and the male is furniture, and pay follows accordingly. What's more, male actors regularly find themselves the unwilling cause of production delays, and reap as a result the irritation and scorn of their peers. Habitual apprehension creates more problems, and this career-destroying pressure eventually destroys every career. Has-beens shuffle into backstage work, or, if they're lucky, marry a female star who can support them.

Yes, they do marry. The strangest aspect of Faludi's portraits is the impulse toward normalcy. Jeff Stryker, who fought to win custody of his son, says, "It's my primary everything, protecting this child"; even cable TV is forbidden. Nick East says he's been thinking about quitting the business, and reading the Bible for direction. He tells Faludi, "This is the most intense part," before turning to the Gospel of John. Even in the lonely apartment of T. T. Boy, the table is always set for a family of four, though no one is ever coming to dinner: "I just thought it looked homey."

Faludi finds Austin McCloud and his wife, Dallas, at home in a two-story place in the suburbs, with toys scattered on the floor and the children watching *The Lion King*. For a successful couple like the McClouds, porn is strictly business. Although the business trades in shock and titillation, years spent before the cameras desensitize the participants till production-time is anything but titillating. So workplace conversations have the matter-of-fact tone of those around watercoolers everywhere. On the set, an actor deferentially compliments Austin, saying how much he enjoyed a sex scene with Dallas.

How does a married couple endure this? "We wanted to say that we would just work with each other," Austin says, but that would have cost three-quarters of their jobs. So they made some rules. Austin selects all of Dallas' costars. And she won't kiss anyone but her husband.

The quaintness of this last stipulation points to a deeper truth: trading bodies may become routine, but what happens in the heart retains devastating force. Another porn-star marriage tragically illustrates this principle. Jill was upset when she learned Cal was cheating on her—a distinction that would be comical if we don't stop to ask why the distinction mattered to her. When Cal grew erratic and angry, Jill packed to leave. He was brokenhearted.

"He wanted to have a normal job," Jill says. "And he wanted me to stay at home and have kids and go to church on Sundays." But Cal finally realized that wasn't going to happen. One night he stood in the street outside her house with a gun to his head. "This is for you, babe," he said, and pulled the trigger.

Cal's despair was not over his inability to hoard Jill's body; the sharing of that body, under the lights and on the screen, was his primary source of income. Instead, it was her heart he wanted, and couldn't get.

One lesson we can learn from the porn stars is that sex and eros are not the same thing. Eros, also known as Cupid, was the Greek god whose arrows pierced the heart with longing. In comparison, powerful as it is, sex is superficial and transitory. Eros hooks the soul, powerful, painful, and imperious. Ignore it at your peril.

But ignoring it is what too much contemporary pontificating about sex does. This leads school professionals to think sex education is accomplished with a course in genital mechanics. It leads our pro-choice friends to think that abortion could be made "rare" with an airdrop of condoms. And it leads Hollywood to turn out films of grinding stupidity that substitute hydraulics for intrigue.

As a college film student I watched a grainy copy of *Deep Throat* one night, until it got too boring. As one of my friends said, "I guess it's not a spectator sport." Soon after, I saw Rudolph Valentino's 1926 silent, *Son of the Sheik*. In this camel drama the protagonists are mostly draped, sometimes burdened with drapery, yet the film has an erotic charge that arcs through the years. It has a plot, real characters interacting at a level of smoldering intensity. Viewers were fascinated.

Son of the Sheik was Valentino's last film before his premature death, which set off paroxysms of mourning. Over a hundred thousand women lined the streets for his funeral cortege and some, it is said, died of grief.

Cal's funeral was smaller. Fellow actors worked the crowd, talking up their recent films. "A year from now people will bring up his stage name," said a producer, "and it will be, 'Cal who?'"

Cal who achieved the highest goals the sexual revolution can offer: boy-toy stardom, fame and fantasy, sexual surfeit. Cal who pulled the trigger on his carefully tended body, destroying in a second the product of years of attentive care. Cal who knew all about sex, but was overthrown by eros.

21 | SEX AND SAINTS

WHAT DO YOU THINK about homosexuality? Why do you think it?

Whatever your answer, you're probably in there: *What Christians Think about Homosexuality: Six Representative Viewpoints*. In his book, Larry Holben presents six different ways that Christians look at the homosexual condition, and critiques each from the point of view of the others. It's the perfect volume for people trying to understand what others believe.

You have met Holben's work before; he was the screenwriter for the very intelligent 1979 film about the Holocaust and Corrie Ten Boom, *The Hiding Place*. This book shows similar intelligence, beginning with its organization. The six positions are given labels their adherents might apply: Condemnation, A Promise of Healing, A Call to Costly Discipleship, Pastoral Accommodation, Affirmation, and Liberation. Each position is then asked the same twelve questions, such as, "What is the God-given intent or design for human sexuality?" and "Is there a homosexual 'condition' (orientation) and, if so, what is its cause or origin?" Throughout, Holben tactfully withholds his own opinion: "Why should my judgment carry more weight than that of the many advocates of the various viewpoints I have quoted?"

The foundational question (and Holben's first) is, "What is the ultimate authority upon which any moral judgment regarding homosexuals and/or homosexual acts is to be based?" Who says what's right? If we say "the Bible," how do we handle scholarship offering new interpretations of texts? If it's "by their lives you shall know them," is homosexuality vindicated by adherents who show kindness, gentleness, and charity? Does God's call for justice include homosexuals, and does that call overrule sexual moral laws?

Who says? Holben's personal opinion is that Christians should "accept responsibility for thinking theologically about the major issues . . . we cannot leave serious moral reflection to the clergy or professional scholars." Though rejecting "well-meaning assertive ignorance," Holben would encourage informed laity to wrestle through to their own conclusions.

Though I admire Holben and his work, and recommend this book to anyone studying the range of current opinion, I disagree with this advice. I have more skepticism about the ability of people to think through to unbiased conclusions, less trust in individual wisdom, less confidence in fallen human reason. Though it's our culture's presumption that individuals must devise their own moral code according to their own sincere convictions, I don't think that's a workable plan.

Though it's the prevalent moral advice, "Think for yourself" is a delusion. It isn't possible to think for yourself, in a vacuum removed from outside influences, fashion, and your own desires. Everyone lives in a specific age, and it seeps into consciousness, affecting nearly every thought. We assume we're thinking for ourselves when we agree with whatever Oprah and the *New York Times* are saying.

Alternatively, we can revolt against anything espoused by

prevailing opinion, and become trapped in mere reaction. Suspicious conservatives keep an eye on whatever Hollywood or the evil media propose, and then sing the old Groucho Marx tune, "Whatever it is, I'm against it." But this is as constrained and unfree as slavishly following fashion. Opinion may be a two-way street, but it's still flat. The terms, style, and even topics of debate have been preset, and some concepts are simply not even visible.

When it comes to moral issues, our age provides no categories except rights and justice, oppression and victim-speak. Sexual issues are illuminated only by the bare-bulb glare of banal, compulsory, politicized sexual practice. These issues are seen in genitally reductionist and strangely solitary terms, as if sexual identity is something achieved by a talented soloist, rather than requiring intimate union as a basic condition.

It's futile to defend historic morality in these flat, politicized categories. Many Christians long to celebrate purity rather than nag about code infractions, but lack a public vocabulary to do so; "purity" and "chastity" have become empty vessels. We ourselves barely understand what purity is, and what it meant to Christians before us.

A few years back I read a lengthy collection of lives of the saints, and gradually realized that they all, from the first century till midway through the twentieth, shared a common view of the body. Distressingly, it was a view I could barely grasp. It was as if they could see a distant mountain peak that was to me just a blur. Elements I could discern included joy and serenity, and the invigorating challenge of self-control. Homosexuality was viewed as a matter-of-fact impediment, one example among many, and not an object of special loathing. Instead, they were looking in the other direction, toward something they greatly desired: chastity, a shining object of joy. I could hear themes of the walled garden and of keeping oneself pure, even at the cost of death.

But my own garden I have not kept. Living in an oversexualized culture, I can barely comprehend purity. It is as if the borders of my garden are trampled and destroyed, and I can only walk the edges and imagine what God meant to be there, and what older brothers and sisters in the faith so readily saw and loved.

A narrow-focus fight against homosexuality, couched in Bible proof-texts, misses the point. We need to gain a more comprehensive understanding of the beauty of chastity, and we can begin by admitting that it is something we only dimly understand. Rather than trying to think for ourselves, we should listen to others—listen to the community of faith before us, around the world and through time. They knew something we don't know.

We live in a reckless age, amnesiac and self-fascinated. Welding together fresh opinions in the basement will not solve this problem. We need to take the time to listen to the wisdom of our forebears in faith—and, harder still, need to find the courage to put it into practice. If they are right, in the practice of chastity we will begin to experience a healing joy. Then, perhaps, we'll find the words for it.

22 | WHAT REALLY MOTIVATES "ANTI-GAY" CONSERVATIVES?

AWHILE BACK I WAS INVITED to a strategy meeting to combat the "gay threat to traditional marriage." I went in hopes of getting a better understanding of what my friends see the threat to be. I'm a committed Orthodox Christian, and believe, as my Church teaches, that the goal of every human life is transformation in Christ. Some spiritual disciplines help that process, and some things we do interfere with it, like being angry or greedy. It's my Church's experience that sex outside heterosexual marriage is another one of those things that gets in the way of progress toward union with God.

I believe this is true, but of course, I don't expect people outside my faith to agree. The first conversation we'd need to have is about Jesus Christ; if they're not interested in knowing Him, I'm not surprised that they're not interested in what we think hinders that union. Even for us Orthodox this is a private matter, to be discussed between a person and his or her spiritual director. Why did my friends think it necessary to organize a public response? I wondered what they saw that I didn't.

So I arrived at the meeting room on the appointed morning and looked around to see a thorough mix of gender, age, race, ethnicity, and faith—Protestants, Roman Catholics, Jews, even a representative of Nation of Islam. We were extraordinarily diverse, but there was one thing we all had in common. Each of us was very deeply committed to a religious faith.

As the day wore on and I listened to the speakers, I wasn't getting much closer to understanding. Sure, homosexual activity is a spiritual hindrance for the people involved, but how does it threaten heterosexuals? I tried to picture how a nice male couple living down the street, mowing their lawn and paying their taxes, could damage my marriage. If we were so concerned about defending marriage, why weren't we talking about the most obvious threat: divorce? Wouldn't reform of divorce laws do much more to shore up marriage than busting up gay couples?

And what about promiscuity? If anything undermines the standard of lifelong monogamy, it's cheapened, merchandised sex. Straight promiscuity destroys families more often than the gay sort; on a list of priorities, we should straighten out straights first. If we were gathered, as speakers kept saying, to support "one man, one woman" marriage, why weren't we talking about cheesy strip clubs or divorce-prevention programs?

When it emerged that some Nation of Islam friends could conceivably stretch marriage to "one man, *four* women," I threw up my hands. I came here with an open mind, I told the crowd, but I haven't yet heard evidence that makes sense to me. And if we go out there saying we oppose homosexuality because traditional marriage is composed of one man and up-to-and-including four women, we'll be the laughingstocks we deserve to be.

The problem, I think, was that my friends assumed homosexuality is a political issue. We got used to thinking in political terms during the abortion debates, and with abortion that was justified; the minimum purpose of law is to prevent violence, particularly against children.

But homosexuality, it seems to me, is vastly different. Widespread promiscuity, straight or gay, is dangerous, but I don't see a reason to rank private homosexuality high on the scale of public threats. I'm willing to be convinced, but I haven't been yet.

Look again at that room full of devout people. If you want to understand us, you must understand the central thing that motivates us: we are people of faith. Most ancient faiths reject homosexual contact.

For some people reading that statement, the conclusion is obvious: "Then the faiths must change!" For them the task of each generation is to update ancient beliefs, making them relevant to current needs. Prevalent contemporary analysis is assumed authoritative and competent to critique the past. They question historic faith, not themselves.

But to those of us gathered in that room, such an idea is self-deceptive and self-defeating. We see the faith rather as ancient wisdom, truths attested by people throughout time and around the world. This multicultural affirmation indicates a wisdom higher than we could devise on our own, mentally clouded as we are by our culture's loud and transitory fashions. So we handle this treasury with gratitude and hope to pass it on intact. We seek illumination and healing. We don't want to change the historic faith; we want the faith to change us.

This is the great submerged reef that will continue to shipwreck understanding until we learn to recognize it. It is futile to begin the sexuality conversation with sexuality itself; that skips over the question of where we get the tools by which we *evaluate* sexuality. Beneath it all, we have two vastly different ways of viewing ancient faith, and our press releases are faxed from different floors of the Tower of Babel.

As a person who moved from a pro-choice to a pro-life position,

I always wanted to increase understanding between the two sides, and was a founder of the "Common Ground" dialogue movement. Over the years I saw wonderful things: abortion providers and clinic protesters, PAC leaders and pastors, talked and listened to each other, gave and received forgiveness, formed lasting friendships. I wish that gay activists and conservatives could begin the same healing path. Minds may not be changed, but hearts can be, once prejudice and stereotypes on both sides blow away.

At present we are hampered and thrilled by wild suspicion of each other's motives and beliefs. I hope that someday we can get serious about listening to each other. I can believe that my gay friends are engaging in something spiritually damaging, without asking the law to stop them. They can perceive that my convictions are grounded in an ancient spiritual consensus, not hate. We still won't agree. But perhaps we can understand each other, and continue the conversation with mutual respect.

23 | BORN THAT WAY

AN INTERVIEW IN THE SEPTEMBER 1994 *Heterodoxy* introduced us to a man the homosexual mainstream (or "Gaystream") would prefer we didn't meet: Leland Stevenson. Stevenson is a spokesman for the North American Man–Boy Love Association, which promotes sexual encounters between adults and adolescent boys.

This organization causes the Gaystream some awkward moments. When reporter Paul Mulshine phoned a representative of the National Gay and Lesbian Task Force, the representative, Ms. Kane, stated that her organization did not support NAMBLA. Then she added, apparently automatically, "We believe that people should not be denied their civil rights because of the sexual orientation with which they are born."

Mulshine stopped her there. "NAMBLA makes that exact same argument. They say pedophiles are born with their sexual orientation. Why should they be deprived of their civil rights?"

"I think I'm going to get off the phone now," said Ms. Kane.

The question of whether people are "born with their sexual orientation" has often been presented as the defining issue of homosexual rights. If "this is the way God made me," proponents say, it's nobody else's business. Conservatives usually counter that sexual preference is not inborn, it's a choice, and so deserves no special protection.

But watch how many ways the question can fall apart. In the first place, there's the NAMBLA problem, which causes even gay activists to feel that there should be some limits on how sexuality is expressed. Men with teen boys is worrisome enough; what if someone claimed he was born with a craving for five-year-old girls? Or could only be satisfied if the partner was terrified? Body-hungers can lead in all sorts of directions; if the context is not sex but anger, it can mean abuse or murder. If we establish a principle that "Bodily impulses cannot be denied," we court all kinds of trouble.

But similar illogic plagues the conservative side. Since when do we believe that, because a behavior is chosen, it shouldn't be legally protected? Christians want to be allowed to keep a Bible on their desk at work, or to homeschool their kids. But if these are mere choices, not genetic compulsions, are they not worthy of protection? That's another questionable premise.

Here's a complication from an entirely different direction. Some lesbians insist that they *weren't* "born that way." A time-honored feminist slogan is, "Biology is not destiny." That means that women aren't biologically compelled to be housewives and moms; they can be astronauts and firefighters too. By the same token, these activists would say, biology does not compel our sexuality. We can choose whom we love; we are pro-choice.

"I've known many women who became homosexual to make a political statement," a gay male friend told me. "I've never known a man who did." It seems like female homosexuality simply has a different, and much less compulsive, quality than male homosexuality. For some men it feels overwhelming, life-long, and unalterable. Women, it seems, can alter. Everyone knows someone who left a heterosexual marriage and became a lesbian. It doesn't surprise us when a woman changes sides. When people think about the in-eradicability of homosexual preference, they're usually thinking about men, not women. And some lesbians would insist on that freedom from "biological destiny."

The inborn-or-chosen question is finally moot. If these things aren't written in our genes, they're so entrenched that they might as well have been. Heterosexuals should admit that we, too, have pref-erences; by adolescence we consistently lean toward tall or short, blond or brunet, slim or hefty. We might puzzle over why we like what we do. But if commanded to change—if told, "It is an abomi-nation to like people with red hair, you should only be attracted to people with brown hair," we'd be at a loss. Even if we wanted to comply, we wouldn't know how to begin. These preferences are in a locked file cabinet, and we can't open them up and move things around.

Once I was talking with a friend after a meeting, and I was surprised when she commented that a young man who had made a presentation was handsome. I hadn't noticed him at all.

Here's what specifically won her admiration: "He was tall, a real Saul, standing head and shoulders over everyone else in the room." I peered up at her, wondering why anyone would consider height to be a plus. Some tall people are very nice, of course, but their faces are too high. You look up and it's Land of Nostrils up there. They have to stoop over awkwardly to give a hug or hold a con-versation. It seems like a disadvantage to me, though they bear it very well.

No, for as long as I can remember it was short, dark, and brainy for me. My teen-years dreamboat was singer Paul Simon, 5'3" with enough brains to make any girl swoon. All through dating years I only liked the short guys, and I could have used all the "Gaystream" lines: I've been like this ever since I can remember. It's not something

I chose. Maybe I was born this way. I can't imagine what it would take to change.

But here's the point. This preference doesn't entitle me to keep a harem of short, brainy guys. Whether desires spring from choice or compulsion, we are still bound to self-control. Strong desire is not a "Get out of the rules free" card. It speaks with a commanding voice, but not the voice of God.

For the sake of argument let's grant that, for some people, homosexuality is inborn. Likewise, history suggests that many heterosexual men are "born with" an impulse to philander. Yet healthy societies have always asked them to restrain themselves, for the sake of the common good, for protection of wives and preservation of families. Fire is good in the fireplace; sex within marriage deepens bonds of love and sends the human race forward one more generation. Fire outside the fireplace may feel just as intense, but it is fraught with danger.

Those who struggle with such passions deserve our prayers. It is naïve and unkind to deny how strong sexual hunger can be. Overcoming these desires and practicing sexual continence requires a kind of heroism. Treating gays with disgust doesn't help them. There's a chance our kindness and encouragement might, as we see that we have sins too. For the struggling gay man, as for the glutton craving chocolate, there is a single rule: if you fall, pick yourself up, and keep going.

For some homosexuals, persistence and prayer may be blessed with healing and a change of inner direction. For others, there will be the difficult life-long discipline of celibacy. Does that sound lonely? The path, in fact, is crowded; gays are few compared with all the heterosexuals who never found a mate, who took monastic vows, who were divorced or widowed, who lived with a sick or disabled or rejecting spouse. More people than we suspect are living celibate lives, and doing it with quiet nobility. Those in a faith community who carry no such burden should be alert to those who do, and regularly offer opportunities for companionship. A "holy kiss" or a hug is also a good idea. It may be that no one else has touched them in kindness all week.

Sixteen hundred years ago St. John Chrysostom wrote, "Even if lust makes imperious demands, if you occupy its territory with the fear of God, you have stayed its frenzy." The final issue is not inborn urges, but behavior. Passions may not be chosen, but actions are.

24 | MONSTER

"I RECOILED SO MUCH from what I had done that it seemed to be not my choice at all. A mystery, I thought. A monster did it."

Michael Warner writes these words in the *Village Voice* (January 31, 1995), in an article titled "Why Gay Men are Having Risky Sex." He is perplexed at the statistics: 30–38% of HIV-negative gay men admit they don't always use condoms. In San Francisco, rates of new infection have nearly quadrupled since 1987. This is not the result of ignorance; pro-condom messages have so saturated the culture that they turn up everywhere but fortune cookies. Warner quotes one activist: "Everybody's grandmother knows about [male homosexual] sex and condoms."

The strategy ever since 1983 has been, "Get the information out and make it attractive. But over and over I hear the same thing from prevention workers: information alone is no longer doing the job." Then Warner found that it wasn't doing the job for him, either. "When I had an unsafe encounter last winter, I spooked myself blank."

Over the course of a longish article, Michael Warner tries to sort this out. Why did he—why do so many homosexual men— risk their lives when they know better? Why isn't it enough just to tell people the right thing to do?

Some will recognize this as an ancient theological question, explored with particular pointedness in Romans 7. But Warner writes from a world that has no history before the Stonewall riots, and no resources beyond its own wit, passion, and fading beauty. "In the vast industry of AIDS education and prevention, I knew of nothing that would help me answer this question." Warner is writing in the pages of an overflowing tabloid weekly; its back pages are tiled with tiny ads offering every imaginable sexual vice, and some unimaginable ones. His article is surrounded with vanity ads for body piercing, hair weaving, muscle gyms and spiritual candy ("Enjoy a past life regression, $39"). In this confused and rootless space, Warner tries to fathom the depth of human self-destruction.

He comes up with several answers: the generalized despair of the homosexual life, the thrill of taunting death ("no sublimity without danger"), the weariness of a constantly monitored sex life and the use of drugs to silence that monitor. There is the deadly variation on "If you loved me you would . . ." this time ending, "trust me when I tell you I'm not sick."

Warner also reports a sad, surprising phenomenon: healthy homosexuals can feel envy for the enhanced identity of the HIV-positive. These do not necessarily appear sick; they may be asymptomatic for many years (when Warner looked up his impulse-partner, he found the man had died of AIDS "only a month after I last saw him, healthy and beautiful as ever"). HIV-positive men are members of a privileged sub-society, those who can live as if there were no tomorrow. They have their own style, their own "mordant humor," their own magazines, like *Diseased Pariah News*. Homosexuals not lucky enough to have HIV may want to try on the identity, just this once.

But the most startling passage in Warner's analysis is this: "The appeal of [homosexual] sex, for many, lies in its ability to violate the responsibilizing frames of good, right-thinking people. AIDS education, in contrast, often calls for people to affirm life and see sex as a healthy expression of self-esteem and respect for others. One campaign from the San Francisco AIDS Foundation urges men to treat sex the way you might buy municipal bonds: 'Playing it safe, making a plan, and sticking to it.' Most efforts to encourage us to take care of ourselves through safer sex also invite us to pretend that our only desire is to be proper and good. Abjection continues to be our dirty secret." If this is the case, "The emphasis on self-esteem . . . may be counter-productive."

Ultimately, homosexuals are refusing to use condoms because they've been told it's the right thing to do. Being good runs counter to their culture. This is a scary monster, but a similar monster lurks in every human heart, unrelated to sexual orientation. This is the monster that every faith and every worldview based on "the basic goodness of humanity" underestimates with deadly regularity. By the grace of God, our pet sins may not be acted out in such life-threatening ways, but they all deserve the same wages. We don't need self-esteem. We need a Savior.

25 | HOTEL FULL OF COWBOYS

WE HAD GATHERED, about a hundred pro-family leaders, for a weekend conference in a Washington hotel. It was encouraging to see so many other fellow laborers assembled at one time; we filled a small dining room at lunchtime, and felt like the forward edge of a mighty army.

But as the day went on, we began to be outnumbered by cowboys. Cowboys in the elevators, cowboys in the halls, cowboys sitting at tiny glass tables in the lounge. Two things about this seemed unusual: first, Washington, DC, is not a cowboy kind of town. Any cows who make it inside city limits have already been reduced to steak. And the bull-byproduct the town is known for is actually produced by guys in suits.

But something else about these cowboys seemed out of synch. I always imagined cowboys to have a sprawling presence scaled for endless plains, a physical expansiveness unrelated to their body size. Cowboys might appear awkward under roof, perhaps charmingly bashful, but never brittle or edgy.

These cowboys didn't fit that image. They were nervous. Their presence was, if anything, smaller than average, more compressed and self-protective. I stood near one waiting at the elevator bank:

perfect black boots, jeans aged carefully as wine, and above the black moustache eyes darting sidewise furtively.

The mystery became clear when I examined the sign over their registration table: Atlantic States Gay Rodeo Association. Back in our meeting room, whispers went hissing by: "All those cowboys—they're homos!" Someone snickered. Someone said, "Maybe we should pray for them." Another grumped, "Next time, we ought to find out who else is going to be in our hotel." But I was thinking about George.

I met George during my pagan college days; I still remember his large, lightbulb-shaped head topped with sparse blond hair, his invisible blond moustache, the compressed and awkward way he carried his large frame. His skin was pale as cellar vines, and his eyes pale as water, barely blue. George was from a hard-scrabble Southern town called Ulmer. George was a genius. George was gay.

One night George and I sat under a tree in the women's quad and he asked me, nervously, if it showed that he was gay. No, I lied. He wasn't effeminate, but he was jittery, arch, and unhappy. Behind his nervous laugh, woundedness flowed out of him like a stream.

Too-clever George had been misunderstood in Ulmer. He grew up dirt-poor, brushing flies away from the peaches at a roadside stand, while reading all eleven volumes of the Durants' *Story of Civilization*. At home he listened to the symphony crackling over the radio from the big city, the county seat. He taught himself some Bach on the piano.

"That boy has no *common* sense," neighbors said. But George had plenty of other kinds of sense: When assigned a paper on paradoxical novelist John Barth, he wrote a hundred pages—cleverly constructed to begin refuting itself on the fiftieth page. (This was in the pre-computer 1970s, when a hard copy was the only kind possible.) He showed me another paper, this one for history, on which the professor had written, "I really am not capable of grading this." George ended up going into Classical Studies, spending Sundays in the library with moldering leather volumes of ancient Greek and Latin.

The sad cowboys reminded me of George. One quiet evening, in a tentatively self-revealing mood, he told me about the loneliness of the gay life. He described the previous weekend's after-hours session at Midge's Bar. Midge's was egalitarian: some nights were set aside for male gays, some for lesbians, and friendly straights were welcome to drop in anytime. Anytime, that is, except Fridays after midnight. Then the doors were closed to give the guys a chance to be alone together, to dress up and stand in the spotlight, lip-synching to scratchy records.

The previous Friday, George said, a chubby guy in a black thrift-shop gown had taken the microphone and stood alone to sing along with *West Side Story*. "There's a place for us, somewhere a place for us," he silently mouthed, behind the female singer's soaring voice. "Someday, somehow, we'll find a new way of living. We'll find a way of forgiving, somewhere."

By the time he finished, everyone was crying. "That's what it's like," George said. "There's no place for us. We never fit in. We don't belong anywhere. All we have is this few hours in a crummy dive on Friday night. Mostly, we're alone."

George gave me the best gift of my life: he introduced me to Gary, my husband now for many years. We planned that, at our wedding out in the woods, George would walk before us in the procession. But a month before that date, George was driving alone down a two-lane North Carolina road. Just outside Rockingham he drifted into the oncoming lane, swerved back to avoid hitting another car, and flipped over into a ditch. He was killed instantly.

Now he is gone, lost forever. Weeds long ago swarmed over the gravel on an Ulmer grave. I will never see him again. Outside an extraordinary extension of God's grace, I have no reason to hope that George was saved. He died just before noon on a warm Good Friday. As far as I can know, he will never see Easter morning.

There is a place for him. There was a place for him.

The sad, nervous cowboys shuffled near us all weekend; we passed by them as Christians, destined for eternity, destined to live for the praise of God's glory. We found them frightening, or humorous, or loathsome. They didn't find us at all.

One of George's favorite quotes was a line from French poet Paul Valery: *"Dieu a tout fait de rien, mais le rien perce."* I was a non-believer, an anti-believer then; I was flippant and cynical and loved it. On a lark I embroidered it as a gift for him, flowing letters festooned with flowers. The translation is: "God made everything out of nothing, but the nothing still shows through." That was the only thing I ever told George about God.